52 WAYS
TO MOTIVATE YOUR STAFF

For a complete list of Management Books 2000 titles,
visit our web-site on http://www.mb2000.com

52 WAYS TO MOTIVATE YOUR STAFF

Trish Nicholson

2000

First published in 1988 by Mercury Books
This revised edition published in 2001 by Management Books 2000 Ltd
Forge House
Limes Road
Kemble
Cirencester
Gloucestershire GL7 6AD
tel: 01285 771441/2
fax: 01285 771055
E-mail: m.b.2000@virgin.net

Printed and bound in Great Britain by Biddles, Guildford

British Library Cataloguing in Publication Data is available ·
ISBN 1-85252-378-6

Introduction

The theme throughout this book is that the prime outcome of staff development is not new knowledge but better action. The objectives of training and development should be those of the workplace – increased effectiveness, performance and output. Unless the aims, content and methods of training are determined by what needs to be achieved at work, you will find yourself in the position of revving up a car engine without being in gear – it sounds good at the time but it doesn't get you anywhere.

Managers at every level of an organisation need to know how to develop their staff through the daily routines of work. For too long, management training has been a cult subject hedged around by the jargon of business schools and bearing little relevance to the harsh realities of work. The emphasis has been too much on systems and controls, and not enough on how to develop people, the major resource of any enterprise, however hi-tech. All performance ultimately depends on human skills and motivation working in unison. Like the old song about love and marriage, you can't have one without the other, and it takes a lot of hard work to keep them together.

In-company training departments have fallen into the same trap of pushing numbers through training programmes. Managers themselves have perpetuated this by not recognising their responsibility for developing their own staff, and being only too keen to leave to others the messy business of getting close enough to people to develop them.

A great deal has been written on the need for industry to invest in more training. This does not automatically result in more learning, nor, more importantly, in better performance unless line managers take part. There are three fundamental reasons why successful staff development has to be manager-driven.

Firstly, no training is value-free. The values, attitudes and assumptions of trainers underpin the content and method of their training. Values make up the why and how of company objectives. If the underlying values of training are not wholly compatible with those of the workplace, the result is frustration and disruption. Even in-company courses can become divorced from the culture down the line if managers are not closely concerned with them, and trainers see themselves only as 'catalysts', unchanged by what is going on in the company both at strategic level and at the workbench.

Secondly, without the full co-operation of line managers, the transfer of their subordinates' newly acquired knowledge and skills to the way they actually do their jobs is often impossible. Training in specialised skills or in personal behaviour may best be achieved away from work, where mistakes can be made in a supportive environment. But to transfer this type of learning to the workplace requires a partnership between trainer, manager and subordinate to ensure opportunities for practice, coaching and feedback. Without this type of integration, money spent on training, however well designed, is an investment with a negative return.

Thirdly, performance can only be improved and maintained if learning, change and development are part of the culture of an organisation. This requires the creation of a learning environment, in which the encouragement of self-development, and learning from colleagues, bosses and subordinates is an expected and continuous process. This environment can only be achieved by those who manage the work of others, from the supervisor to the chief' executive.

It is for these managers that this book has been written, partly to enable them to get a better return from their company's investment on trainers and courses, but primarily to help them develop the skills and knowledge to create a learning environment in which employees are developed as a way of working. The development of other people's potential depends on good leadership, but there is no section headed 'leadership skills' - they are implicit in every chapter.

It is a book of practical ideas to be dipped into, and is the result of my experience as both a trainer of managers and a manager of trainers. Some of what is written may already be familiar, but I hope at least that it may put a new slant on old themes and suggest some fresh approaches.

Acknowledgements

To Nick Nicholson (who bought me my first typewriter too many years ago), for believing I would one day make good use of it; to numerous friends, colleagues and students, for inadvertently contributing to many of the thoughts and ideas in this book by asking the right questions; to Donald John MacKay, Richard Cameron and Roger Paine, for reading and commenting on the first draft; to my past bosses, for teaching me much of what I know about staff development (good and bad); to my work team, Tom Riddell, Richard Beagent, Irene Whyte and Angela Bremner, for teaching me the rest – I extend my sincere thanks. Without all of you this book would not have been written – but I don't hold you responsible!

CONTENTS

INTRODUCTION 5
Bridging the gap between management and staff development.
Training is no longer a cult subject owned by trainers. The
purpose of staff development is better action and increased
performance. Why managers must control this process and
learn how to develop staff through work.

ACKNOWLEDGEMENTS 7

1: KNOW YOURSELF 15
The effects of our attitudes and behaviour upon others. How to
become aware of our own style and potential for varying our
behaviour when dealing with different people to assist their
development.

2: KNOW YOUR STAFF 21
We need to know people as whole persons in order to develop
them to their full potential, and yet our perception of them is
limited without making special efforts. Ways of getting to know
your staff better.

3: MATCH PEOPLE AND JOBS 24
Performance is not always related to ability. Defining activity
preferences and using them to get the right people in the right
jobs and increase job satisfaction.

4: LEARN HOW PEOPLE LEARN 27
Experience alone without feedback and guidance leads at best
to survival rather than development. How to help people learn
from experience by understanding and using their different
learning styles.

5: COMMUNICATE EFFECTIVELY 32
We must understand and break through the barriers to effective
communication in order to use staff development techniques.
How Transactional Analysis can help this process.

6: INDUCT NEW RECRUITS 38
Employee development begins on their first day. How to ensure
the best induction programme before they even arrive, and
develop the rest of your team at the same time.

7: PAY ATTENTION TO YOUR STAFF 42
People who are taken for granted don't develop. How to make your presence felt and let your staff know you notice and appreciate them without losing time on the job.

8: DELEGATE FOR DEVELOPMENT 44
Delegation is an essential skill for good management; with a little additional planning and purpose it can be a very powerful tool for developing staff potential.

9: COACH 48
The essential skills for effective coaching. How to find the time and the situations to increase learning and improve performance.

10: GIVE CREDIT 53
The power of recognition, and the importance of letting others have credit when it is due – not just to the individual, but by making it known openly.

11: GIVE FEEDBACK 56
Feedback is essential to personal and professional development. How to give positive and negative feedback and still remain on good terms.

12: USE MENTORING 59
The use of peers and/or subordinates out of the direct line of command as a source of staff development, and how this develops both the mentor and the mentored.

13: PREPARE FOR PROMOTION 62
How to develop people for the next rung of the ladder while providing a reward system for results, and assessing ability. How to help 'stuck' middle managers.

14: CREATE EXCHANGES AND SECONDMENTS 65
The value to the organisation and the individual of wider experience. How to set up and maintain exchange relationships with other organisations and between sectors.

15: ENRICH JOBS 68
Variety and new challenges provide a source of development as well as means of assessment. How to avoid rigidities in job descriptions and increase job satisfaction.

16: STRETCH ABILITIES 72
Most jobs only use part of our potential. How to stretch people in their jobs by applying their other talents to work in new ways.

Contents

17: TAKE CALCULATED RISKS   75
Don't smother people, and don't make mistakes a 'hanging offence'. Learn to take calculated risks and teach your team to do the same, while ensuring they learn from the experience.

18: USE PROJECT TEAMS   78
How staff can develop from participating in cross-departmental project teams. How to set them up and get the best training value from them.

19: ENCOURAGE LEARNING FOR ACTION   84
What is 'Action Learning'? How to create self-sustaining learning 'sets' to enable staff to learn from mutual problem-solving in real time, on real problems and improve their decision-making.

20: CONSIDER QUALITY CIRCLES   90
How they work and the ways in which they can develop employees as well as the product. Considerations in assessing their use in your organisation and how to set them up.

21: BE FLEXIBLE   95
How rigid attitudes such as stereotyping, clock-watching, and recruiting clones prevent staff development, and how to overcome them.

22: STIMULATE CREATIVITY   98
How to develop and encourage in your team the desire and opportunity to be both creative and innovative in solving problems and pursuing opportunities.

23: ENCOURAGE PERSONAL DEVELOPMENT   103
How personal development differs from skills and knowledge training. What to do to encourage it and gain valuable spin-off for the organisation as well as the individual.

24: CAREER PLAN   108
Paying attention to an individual's career progression can speed his or her development, make the best use of talents, and retain good people in the organisation.

25: USE THE TRAINER   112
How to make the best use of the training staff in your organisation to get what you want, when and where you want it, for your team and yourself.

11

26: PLAN TRAINING AND DEVELOPMENT 115
Ad hoc requests to go on courses may turn out to be a waste of money. How to identify training/development needs systematically, and plan a strategy to implement them.

27: RECORD PROGRESS 121
How to discuss and record training and development progress with staff, which in itself contributes to the development process.

28: INTEGRATE OFF-THE-JOB TRAINING 1214
When off-the-job training is necessary, how to ensure that the learning is reinforced and applied on the job with pre-course briefing, debriefings and joint action plans.

29: LEARN TO INSTRUCT 128
Simple hints on how to give one-to-one, or small group instruction yourself, where and when you want it, without being a pedagogue.

30: USE VISUAL AIDS TO COMMUNICATE 131
Simple but effective visual aids for use in instruction, team briefings, or presentations, for you and your staff.

31: BRIEF YOUR TEAM 134
The staff development to be gained from regular briefing meetings with your team by sharing leadership, using brainstorming and allocating specific tasks on behalf of the group.

32: KEEP UP TO DATE 137
How to help staff to keep up to date with professional/technical knowledge and contacts even when time is short – and keeping yourself up to date at the same time.

33: ENCOURAGE MUTUAL SUPPORT 140
Manage conflict before it becomes a destructive force that prevents development. How to encourage mutual support and help your team to develop each other.

34: SOCIALISE 144
Why socialisation is important at work, and how to use the process for better performance and employee development.

35: LISTEN 147
To develop subordinates requires effective communication and interpersonal skills – the key to these is listening. How to listen with the eyes as well as the ears to understand non-verbal as well as verbal messages.

36: COUNSEL   150
Counselling techniques for managers. How to use them to
remove barriers to development and assist personal growth as
well as create better working relationships.

37: APPRAISE FOR DEVELOPMENT   156
How to overcome the inadequacies of formal annual appraisal
systems and use them to develop those who report to you
without falling out with the personnel department.

38: INFORM AND INVOLVE   161
The importance of quality as well as quantity of information in
developing staff and gaining commitment. How to beat the
grapevine and get development value out of briefing groups.

39: RESPECT YOUR TEAM   166
Respect not only their right to hold and express opinions, and
to be themselves, but their time too, if you want them to respect
you and your time.

40: ENCOURAGE ASSERTIVENESS   169
Why assertive behaviour between you and your staff is
important for development and of value to the rest of the
organisation. How to develop assertiveness in your management
style for yourself and those who report to you.

41: LEARN FROM YOUR SUBORDINATES   175
When and how to learn from subordinates while maintaining
your position and developing their technical, communication
and leadership skills.

42: CREATE A LEARNING ENVIRONMENT   178
How to create an environment in which everyone exercises
their ability to learn and to teach so that all forms of training
are applied effectively in practice, in a more adaptive and
vigorous organisation.

43: EVALUATE TRAINING AND DEVELOPMENT   181
The importance of evaluating your own development activities
as well as formal training courses and how to go about it.

44: MANAGE STRESS   185
What causes stress and how it can prevent development. How
to manage it, and help your staff to do so, in a way that
develops their stress threshold.

45: COMMAND YOUR TIME   191
Developing staff is a time-consuming activity, but if you want
results it is a top priority. How to gain command of your time
while developing your staff in the process.

46: DEVELOP YOURSELF   196
To be able to develop and extend others it is necessary to
maintain your own capacity for change and development – even
if you're the chief executive. How to recognise and implement
your own development needs.

47: IMAGE BUILD   201
How to create the right image for staff development both within
your department and to others in the organisation, which your
team will be proud to be part of and contribute to.

48: MANAGE YOUR BOSS   204
Developing your staff depends on a good relationship with your
boss. How to understand and influence your boss to support
your training and development strategy.

49: SMILE OFTEN   208
Work can be fun, and smiling is an essential tool to assertiveness.
Smile often and you have to do less to control unwanted behaviour.

50: BE AN EXAMPLE   210
The hardest thing about being a good manager is that unless
you live the values you try to impart, they will not take root in
others. How to develop staff by example.

51: KNOW (AND SHARE) THE CUSTOMER   213
The dangers of limiting your horizons to your team. Ways to
keep you and your team in touch with your customers and clients.

52: READ A CHAPTER EVERY WEEK   216
Learning needs reinforcement or else good ideas fall by the
wayside. Use these chapters to remind yourself of things you
meant to do. Are you doing them? Are they working?

SOME USEFUL ADDRESSES   218

INDEX   220

1

Know Yourself

A quotation from Robert Burns' poem, 'To A Louse', has become very famous:

> *0 wad some Pow'r the giftie gie us*
> *To see oursels as others see us!*

But the next line, for some reason, is usually forgotten and yet it is significant because self-knowledge is not sought from pure vanity but for very practical reasons, especially for a manager:

> *It wad frae mony a blunder free us...*

Management is about encouraging and controlling the behaviour of others. We cannot do that unless we understand, encourage and control our own behaviour first; and if we wish positively to develop the attributes of those whom we manage, then self-knowledge is even more important.

The two basic reasons for this are that:

- Attitudes and prejudices learned throughout our lives, sometimes in totally different contexts, influence what we do and say now, even without our knowing it.
- What we do and say can have lasting impact upon others, and usually determines the response we get in return.

One of the greatest influences on how we behave to other people is the image we have of ourselves, which acts as a filter, interpreting all the other information our senses feed to us.

Zen Buddhists understand very well that dealing effectively with the outside world begins with understanding ourselves, and there is a simple little story which graphically portrays this.

Wandering disciples of Zen can claim food and shelter from any Zen temple if they initiate and win an argument on Buddhism.

Late one evening a travelling monk arrived at a temple where two brothers lived. The elder was very clever, but the younger was rather stupid and had only one eye. The elder brother was tired from much study and told his younger brother to meet their visitor, but advised him to request the discussion be in silence. The traveller and the younger brother went off together to the shrine.

A few minutes later the visitor sought out the elder brother to tell him that the young man had so cleverly beaten him in argument that he would have to leave and seek shelter elsewhere.

'Tell me what happened' said the elder brother.

The visitor explained: 'I held up one finger representing Buddha, the enlightened one. He held up two fingers signifying Buddha and his teachings. So I held up three fingers to represent Buddha, his teachings and his followers in harmony. 'Then he shook his clenched fist in my face indicating that all three come from one realisation.'

Just as the wandering monk had gone on his way, the younger brother came rushing in, angry with the discourteous treatment he had received at the hands of the visitor.

His brother asked him what had taken place.

'No sooner had he sat down than the boorish fellow insulted me by holding up one finger, drawing attention to the fact that I have only one eye. Responding with constraint and courtesy, I held up two fingers, congratulating him on his two eyes. He then insulted me again by holding up three fingers indicating that between us we had only three eyes. I lost my temper at this point and went to punch him in the face but he got up and left.'

There are many employees who seem to interpret every action by management as a two-fingered gesture, and there are many managers who react to employees in the same way. Most of the time, it is a self-fulfilling prophecy, based on the expectation of the response – an expectation conditioned by attitudes which may be quite erroneous, but which seem to 'prove' themselves whenever the reaction is repeated. It's a bit like the 'when did you stop beating your wife?' question. If you expect people to be bloodyminded and approach them accordingly, they are almost bound to respond in the way you expect, because you haven't given them much option.

Feeling bad about other people is usually a reflection of feeling bad about ourselves. We begin to learn our own sense of worth from our earliest contacts with parents, guardians, neighbours, friends, teachers – anybody we come in contact with – depending on how they behave towards us. At the same time, we establish feelings about them as individuals, which become generalised as feelings towards 'people'.

'People can't be trusted.' 'People don't like me.' 'People only work if you make life tough for them.' 'If you're nice to people, they trample all over you.' These are some reactions. 'People are pretty helpful.' 'I get along with most people.' 'Most people will do a good job if you get them interested in it.' 'If you treat people right, they'll treat you right.' These are others.

In 1970, an American psychiatrist, Thomas A Harris, wrote a best seller on this theme. It was called *The Book of Choice*, but has since been published as *I'm OK – you're OK*. He was no transcendental west-coast 'shrink', but spent most of his career in the hard reality of the US Navy, where objectives had to be achieved – and usually in a hurry.

Using his work, it is possible to identify and map out the position from which we view life, based on the image we have of ourselves and others acquired through childhood learning, as in Figure 1.1.

You're OK

'I'm sure you didn't mean to do it wrong. It's my fault for asking you. I never seem to do things right.'	'It's not like you to make a mistake like this; let's work on the problem together and we'll fix it.'

'I'm not OK' ──────────────┼────────────── **'I'm OK'**

'You're really no good at this are you? I shouldn't have given it to you. I shall never sort it out now.'	'You've really fouled things up this time. Give it to me. I never have any problem with this.'

'You're not OK'

Figure 1.1

Which remark from the figure do you use when a mistake is made by your subordinates? Your children? Your partner? Your garage mechanic?

Managers with the life position 'You're OK – I'm OK' feel good about themselves and about their subordinates. As a result, a mistake is a learning opportunity which does not threaten but develops the employee, and cements the relationship for the future.

The 'I'm OK-you're not OK' manager has a good opinion about his or her own abilities, but tends to build up his/her image by putting other people down. This manager's subordinates are unlikely to admit mistakes in this relationship, and will certainly never learn and develop as a result of them. Mistrust becomes mutual, and when the subordinate tries to hide a mistake, or corrects it ineffectively without guidance, it will reinforce the manager's attitude that the subordinate is no good.

The good news from Thomas A Harris is that, once we are aware of all this, we can change it. We don't have to be locked into our early learning – it was learnt and so can be unlearnt if we recognise it and want to do something about it. A good boss will want to develop an 'I'm OK-you're OK' relationship with his or her people for reasons which are central to effective management and good results:

- It leads to better judgements when making decisions about delegation, promotion, or recruitment.
- It develops trust not only between boss and subordinate but within the team or department as a whole, and trust is the basis of good management as well as staff development.
- It encourages realistically high expectations of a person's ability, which are more likely to be met.
- It enables coaching and counselling to be carried out positively and effectively without judgement.
- It enables honest appraisals of performance to be made, and they can lead to genuine improvement and justified reward.
- It creates the kind of relation in which boss and subordinates can share the same values and aim for the same goals.
- It makes life a lot more satisfying for everyone.

As I feel good about me, and I also feel good about you, let's work together and look at some things you can do to increase awareness of your own life position, and ways you can change it if you wish.

☑ Keep a detailed diary for a couple of days of what you say to people and the responses you get. Analyse these statements on the basis of 'Who is OK?'. Identify a trend and for a further week, concentrate on recording the situations or the kind of statements that made the trend. If they are 'I'm OK – you're OK' statements – great! If not, rephrase them until they are, and consciously use them when those situations arise again. The statements should gradually change the reactions you get from people, and confirm the 'You're OK' outlook. You may have to persevere if you or they have been 'not OK' for a long time – if you can share with them what you are trying to achieve, all the better.

☑ Confide what it is you are trying to do to someone you can trust, and get them to help you to identify your life position from your interactions with them. Don't indulge in 'navel gazing', stick to the facts of what you say and do, because those are the things you can start to change straight away if you want to.

☑ Next time you have a few minutes to spare, waiting for a train, lying in the bath, or sitting in the dentist's waiting room, make a list of all your good qualities and skills – don't stop until you reach at least a dozen. Then draw up a similar list for one of your subordinates, then for another, then for your closest friend or partner. If you are married, the acid test is to do the same for your in-laws – remember, don't stop until you reach at least a dozen!

☑ After a significant interaction with one of your subordinates or your boss, e.g. discussing a project, sorting out an error, or briefing for delegation, give yourself five minutes' reflection time to go over the conversation and ask yourself why you each said the things you did -try to identify motives and life positions, and note anything you want to do differently next time. Plan how and when you will do it.

☑ Be aware of non-verbal communication. It can have even greater impact than words – the scowl, avoidance of eye contact and dismissive hand gesture which says 'You're not OK' and the clasped hands, slumped position and averted gaze which says 'I'm not OK'.

☑ Develop the habit of watching out for other people's 'OK' status during meetings, on trains, at family gatherings. Don't get paranoid about it, but being more aware of the games other people are playing will not only help you not to succumb to them but will make you more aware of your own.

☑ Read around the subject a little and discuss it in a general way at coffee break, on the golf course, at the creche. This will increase your familiarity with the idea, while opening up others to the possibilities of working along the same lines. Most of us just don't realise we are sending out 'not OK' messages until someone has the courage to tell us – but the motive has to be a genuine and unselfish interest in the other person's well-being, not an exercise in manipulation.

☑ Once you can work on an 'I'm OK – you're OK' basis comfortably, broaden the scope of your self-knowledge by doing a SWOT analysis. List your Strengths, Weaknesses (you can now do this without feeling 'not OK'), Opportunities and Threats. Work out how you can use the strengths, and the opportunities to lessen the impact of both the weaknesses, and the threats. During this analysis, it is common to find that by the time you get to the second stage, many of the threats seem to have solved themselves, and most of the weaknesses become manageable, especially if you link each weakness directly with a strength that can enable you to overcome it in some way, or to compensate for it when necessary.

What I have written here applies equally to relations with trade union representatives, your bosses, customers, family and friends. But remind yourself from time to time during your journey of self-discovery that achievement is 80 per cent wanting to and 20 per cent sweat!

Resources
If you want to go more deeply into the subject, the following two books are classic texts and very readable: *Games People Play*, E. Berne (Penguin, 1968); and *I'm OK: You're OK*, Thomas A. Harris (Pan, 1973).

2

Know Your Staff

We can't manage what we don't know. Ask any number of bosses if they know their subordinates and they will say of course they do. Do you know your subordinates' birthdays? The names of their children? Important anniversaries in their lives? What date did they join you, get their last promotion, have a major achievement at work or in the community? What are their aspirations for the future?

Priests, ministers and rabbis know the importance of being familiar with details that are significant to the individuals concerned and convince them that you know who they really are. It is common practice for the local parson to keep a little black book in which all the major life events of his parishioners are recorded. Nobody really expects him to remember all these details, but while they don't acknowledge the existence of the little black book either, they are nonetheless filled with warmth and admiration when he calls round to see Mrs Plunket and asks how Annie is getting on at college and whether Simon has got over the measles.

The fact that he has hundreds of parishioners, and most of them don't come to church regularly, does not make this an insincere exercise. The sincerity is in the wish to be in touch with important events in their lives, and to ensure that he is finding out about them and recording them. Motivating dispersed parishioners with no short-term bonus scheme is quite a daunting task.

Keeping a handy note of such details of your staff would at least avoid the embarrassing situation of one boss who welcomed his subordinate into his office for an annual appraisal with the words, 'Ah! come in Keith, how are you?', only to get the response, 'Actually I'm called John; I'm fine, thank you'. Sure enough, 'Keith' was the first name on the form the boss had got from personnel, but the subordinate had always been called by his second name!

Bosses who walk around their patch regularly, stop to chat briefly at coffee time and take a personal interest in their staff don't make this kind of mistake. Even with a small number of staff, it is useful to keep a notebook or a card index

21

of important personal details, interests and major achievements to help you build up a picture of the whole person. Without this positive effort, we see only the tip of the iceberg of each individual.

The better we know people, the easier it is to engage their interest in the work and goals of the department, and to develop their abilities in achieving them. The greatest compliment is to have someone sufficiently interested in you to know something important about you – especially if it is the boss. Such attention to detail also develops relationships and loyalties which can extend to the whole team.

This is the data collection side which, while important, is only part of the story. Getting to know people well depends on being able to communicate with them. This does not just mean talking to them, but listening to them and understanding their point of view whether you agree with it or not. Effective communication, whether verbal or written, always begins with putting yourself in the other person's shoes. To use an American phrase – starting where they are at.

Any managers worth their salt would pride themselves on the professional and technical knowledge of their own field, whether it is computers, engineering, the food industry, or medicine. This is considered an essential part of professional competence. Essential to managerial competence is knowing the human resources you manage as thoroughly as you recognise a sound structure, know your product, or appreciate the intricacies of a lab test.

Reflect for a moment on the following suggestions:

- Your subordinates probably have the same 'hang-ups' and worries that you have.
- They want to get to know you too because they can relate better to someone they can understand as a person.
- ''The boss' is a powerful influence in most people's lives. Almost the first thing they will say when they get home is 'Do you know what the boss said today?'
- Relationships take more than a few minutes at a time to develop. Frequent brief interactions are good to keep you in touch with events, but they are not enough to maintain real contact with people.
- A good boss/subordinate relationship is often the most important factor in job satisfaction.
- The power of shared values as motivators and developers cannot be overestimated, and they can only be transmitted through sound relationships based on mutual knowledge and understanding.

You can't relate to the unknown; and you can't develop what you don't relate to. List the people that report to you. If any one of them was to leave tomorrow and you had to make a presentation to him or her, how much research would you have to do to be able to stand up and talk knowledgeably and meaningfully about the individual and the contribution he or she made to the organisation? If the answer is more than five minutes' thought, you have a lot of catching up to do in getting to know your staff.

3

Match People and Jobs

There are occasions when, despite having tried everything you can think of to develop a subordinate, he or she still seems unresponsive or unmotivated. This may not reflect the ability of the individual, but simply the fact that you have a square peg in a round hole. To continue whittling away at the peg is likely to do no more than produce a chip on the subordinate's shoulder.

Staff development requires a knowledge of all your employees in relation to the work they do, and others with whom they do it. It is only effective if it takes into account the total work context, including the elements which go to make up job satisfaction.

Consistently performing under par, absenteeism and high turnover can all be symptoms of low job satisfaction. However, although having the skills to achieve good results and the recognition of success are both important in maintaining job satisfaction, they may not be enough.

Some recent research has identified strong and enduring attitudes towards work, based not on ability to do it but on preferences for the type of decisions and data that are handled in carrying out the work. Until they were tested, the subjects themselves were not aware of the basis of these preferences nor the implications for their careers.

How people end up in the careers they do is the stuff of anecdotes at the nineteenth hole. It can be as haphazard as accepting the first job that comes along for want of anything else to do, or as predetermined as fulfilling parental expectations under threat of disturbing the entire cosmic order if ignored.

Either way, people can find themselves in a job which they are quite capable of doing, but in which they are dissatisfied and unlikely to develop. This block may be an expression of what the researchers call 'decision preferences'.

They identify two distinct preferences:

- **Qualitative**: associated with decision-making which is intuitive, based on 'gut feel' and an acceptance of handling risk and uncertainty.

- **Quantitative**: associated with calculative decision-making, based on painstaking fact-gathering, analysis and a search for the one right answer.

Each person's preference for one or the other varies in strength, but endures throughout life and is not readily changed. It may even be linked to the structure of the brain, in that the left-hand side of the brain is believed to control sequential thinking, and the right-hand intuitive thinking, and it has long been known that individuals make more use of one side than the other in the way they habitually think.

One major manufacturing corporation was so impressed with the notion that its managers were only using half their faculties that it set up a series of in-house courses called 'Whole Brain Decision Making', as a means of improving decision-making within the corporation.

The real value of this to human resource management, and particularly development, is to analyse job content on the same basis, and compare the results with the preference of the job-holder.

Jobs with high qualitative content are those dealing with people, team work, creativity and uncertainty, e.g. architecture, management, selling, caring professions and teaching. High quantitative content is found in jobs requiring a high degree of precision and certainty, e.g. engineering, accountancy, assembly work, data analysis and laboratory testing.

A person with a high score for a qualitative decision preference is unlikely to feel very satisfied in a job with a high quantitative decision content. The problem may not be one of initial career choice, but may arise when promotion is made to a job with essentially different requirements, e.g. when a successful scientist is put in charge of handling people, or an effective social worker is required to control budgets and resources.

Job satisfaction tends to be higher the further one progresses up the hierarchy. This is partly because at this level there is more scope for adjusting the job to suit personal preference, e.g. by delegation, although it does not necessarily follow that this results in the job being done most effectively for the organisation.

Lower down the hierarchy, this flexibility is usually absent and the effects of being in an unsuitable job are more apparent. Some jobs are of such a routine and mechanistic nature that their quantitative content is greater than scores found for any human being, even those with the highest quantitative preference. If this sort of work really is unavoidable, then developing employees who do it has to begin with ways of reorganising the method of work, so that each job is designed to come within the normal range of preferences, and recruitment is made on that basis.

Awareness of decision preferences can enable you to get a better match between job and post-holder, and to re-examine the effectiveness of some standard development procedures:

- If the only significant reward for success is promotion, then a good performer working within his or her preference may be moved into an area of work for which he or she is basically unsuited.

- A subordinate who is performing less well than expected may develop more successfully if moved to a different job, by lateral transfer, or even promotion.

- Recruitment decisions based too heavily on the candidate's educational achievements or past performance in a different position may result in a mismatch between the basic characteristics of the job and the preference of the candidate. There are far fewer poor employees than there are bad selectors.

- Group performance and problem-solving, in project teams for example, are likely to improve if individual decision preferences are known and understood, and if some matching of preferences within work groups is possible.

- Selecting the most appropriate training course for a particular subordinate should include knowledge of whether the methods of tuition are qualitatively or quantitatively based, and which best suits the subordinate.

- Decision preferences have a strong influence in determining an individual's frame of reference, and an awareness of them can make coaching and career counselling more effective.

- Rather than lose or discard square pegs, it might be of benefit to your organisation to create a few square holes; theirs may be the skills you least tolerate and most need.

One of the most challenging features of staff development is also one of the most rewarding. Because it is about improving the performance not only of the individual, but ultimately of the whole organisation, the boss has to think beyond the person to the job, and beyond the work content to the objectives of the company, i.e. not just at the pegs and the holes, but the board containing the holes as well.

To be really effective, staff development must keep posing and answering the question, What are we all here for?

Resources

Decision Preference Analysis (DPA) was developed by J. C. Kable and R. E. Hicks of Queensland University, Australia, and the diagnostic questionnaire is published in Australia by NIS Associates Pty Ltd.

4

Learn How People Learn

A fractious 2-year-old child was persistently fiddling with the ashtray attached to the seat in front of him while travelling on a bus, despite numerous warnings from his mother that he would hurt himself. Inevitably, a few minutes later he jammed his fingers and yelled with pain and indignation. The exasperated mother merely replied, 'Well, that'll lern yer'.

Grammar may not have been her strong point, but in terms of learning theory she was right. Most of our valuable lessons in life have not been taught; they were discovered by experience. There is a difference between teaching and learning, and the latter does not always follow from the former. Adults learn more effectively when they are in control of the pace and method of learning. They like to see the practical applications while they learn, and they value their own experience, which they want to be able to apply to learning.

Our lives are full of experiences from which we can learn to handle the next situation better. Think for a moment about the variety of experiences you had at work yesterday and identify something you learned from one of them.

We also learn from other people's experience, not just by watching them at work, seeing how the boss runs a difficult meeting or approaches a crisis, but by listening to others talking about their experience. As much learning goes on in the bar after a training course as takes place in the classroom.

If it was just as easy as that, there would be no problem. But experience itself is not enough. It is how we use it that determines whether or not we learn anything, and a lot of people don't. Simply living through experiences shows no more than an ability to survive. In some organisations, that may be an achievement in itself, but it does not necessarily lead to development and improved performance.

To start with, you can help your subordinates to learn more from their experience by:

- giving time for them to review their actions and work out what was effective, what wasn't and why, rather than indulging in constant 'fire-fighting' (it might prevent a few fires)

27

- giving feedback on how they perform; on the results and the way they achieved them
- encouraging them to question their assumptions and ready-made conclusions about what experiences mean
- letting them try new ways of doing things to create fresh experiences, rather than rigidly following previous patterns or adopting other people's solutions as short-cuts.

But enabling people to reach their full learning potential is not as simple as this. Learning is a totally self-generated activity. We can only really develop ourselves. A good boss must therefore stimulate in others the desire to learn, and create a working environment in which learning is possible.

To add to the problem, not everyone learns in the same way. But if you understand what some of these differences are and what they mean, you can gear your management methods to work with them rather than against them.

Learning (and problem-solving) can be seen as a cyclical process of continuing and overlapping activities. It is perhaps easier to visualise from Figure 4.1.

Learning is more effective if we use each stage of the cycle fully. For example, you might have held your first brainstorming session with your team last week. After the experience, you would get feedback from it and then review it in your mind, e.g. 'Was this the

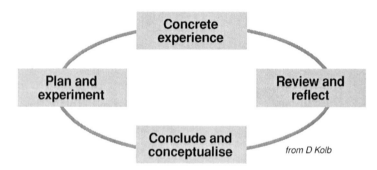

Figure 4.1

only way to achieve what I wanted? Quite a few ideas came out of it, but why was there such a long tense silence at the beginning?' After this period of reflection, you would draw your conclusions about the outcome and the causes, and then conceptualise possible solutions to improve the session, or to use another way of achieving your objective, e.g. 'The method is fine but it is important how it is set up. I should have explained more fully what it was about. They will feel more confident next time'. You then plan and experiment from your conclusions. 'I'll start the next session with coffee and chat, and take part in someone else's session first to get more experience of brainstorming myself.' If you apply what you have learned in the four stages of the process you will get better results next time – even more so if you continue with the cycle after each experience.

Where you start on the cycle in Figure 4.1 depends on the circumstances. We don't always know in advance what experiences we are going to have. When you drive to work in the morning and find yourself struck in a 6-foot snowdrift along with a solid mile of other vehicles, then you're obviously starting with the experience. And you will have plenty of time for reflection!

If you know a problem is looming, e.g. having to speak at a conference, you can start with the theorising and mug up some facts and figures. A well thumbed copy of Hints on Public Speaking is also useful. You can use the entire sequence to make annual appraisals of your staff more of a learning experience for you both, by starting with a factual account of their experience over the year, then reflecting upon it together, drawing conclusions, and so on through the cycle. The same approach can be applied to group projects or individual work assignments which require new skills.

But not everybody is equally adept at using the four stages of the cycle. Some people learn better from 'concrete experience' - just going and doing it – than they do from conceptualisation and theory, for example. That is their 'learning preference'. This does not mean that they can't learn from theory, nor that they have made a conscious decision not to. It is simply that they habitually depend on practical experience for learning and have not developed skills in the other areas. The reasons for this are usually a mixture of their response to formal education, early work experience, personality and natural abilities.

There is some correlation between learning preferences and career choices. Marketing people tend to depend more on concrete experience and experimentation, while production engineers use theory and experimentation. Town planners prefer reflection and conceptualisation, and in personnel and welfare, the common preferences are concrete experience and reflection. Whether the career influences the learning preference, or vice versa, has kept 'conceptualisers' busy for years.

We can consciously develop the learning styles we use less often. The more learning styles we can use, the more effective the learning and the better solutions we produce to problems. If we don't reflect and theorise sufficiently, we are less likely to learn from experience, to repeat mistakes, to continue rigidly with what worked last time without thinking out new approaches, and rush into immediate action ourselves without thought for the rest of the team. If we concentrate too much on reflection and theory, we are likely to get little done and exasperate everyone else in the process.

But you can use the learning preferences of your staff as strengths in the way they learn and work individually, and in groups. For example, you are launching a promotion campaign for a new product on a tight schedule and your team is having to learn more or less as it acts. Give your 'theorist/conceptualiser' the job of researching product specifications and working out a basic strategy for the campaign. Set your 'reflector' on reviewing past campaign performances and observing what competitors are showing in their promotions. Your 'experimenter' should do well discussing with the others the critical path analysis for the various stages of the action, and your 'experiencer' in negotiating the budget allocation and rounding up the resources for the job.

Helping your staff to develop their less preferred learning styles is best not done under pressure; it takes time and lots of feedback, but here are some suggestions. To increase capacity to learn from experience and experimentation get your subordinates to do the following:

- Complete an entirely different type of new task, however small, each week, e.g. arrange a face-to-face discussion with someone they normally only deal with indirectly, change their work area around, park in a different place, change their time or place for lunch – anything to create new experiences.

- Have more contact with people, e.g. let them sponsor a new employee, coach someone in a particular skill, organise the office party, deliver/collect personally urgent reports/correspondence -anything that makes them react to the moment and think on their feet.

- Attend a seminar/exhibition/conference and ask at least one question during a plenary session and report verbally to the team on their return, chair team briefings or other meetings, participate in meetings they don't normally go to, as your substitute.

- Increase the variety in the work they do, and, in particular, undertake tasks jointly with another colleague, or with a group; hold brainstorming sessions with subordinates or colleagues.

To increase capacity to learn from reflection and conceptualisation, get your subordinates to:

- Observe a senior level board or council meeting, at which they cannot speak, and produce a report for you analysing the arguments put forward and the process of discussion; do a review of office/production procedures and draw up proposals for improvements, justifying their recommendations – any activities which encourage logical thought and rational analysis.

- Read articles in professional journals and textbooks on their particular subject and write summaries to up-date you and their colleagues, write a departmental guide for new employees or a news bulletin for the section, or up-date the staff handbook.

- Maintain a learning log and at least twice a week enter a factual description of a significant recent experience, listing the conclusions reached as a result, i.e. about themselves, their skills or their job; then draw up plans of action they intend to implement, including when, how and with whom. Regularly review the log together.

Both programmes will be more effective if you ask regularly about progress and give feedback on the results; and of course you can use similar ideas to develop your own learning styles. Few people have equal skills in all four styles, i.e. are 'integrated learners', but any extension in your learning potential is worth the effort, especially if there are direct spin-offs for work and colleagues, which the above suggestions are intended to provide.

A further use of learning preferences is in the choice of training methods for your staff. Your 'theorist' is unlikely to get the most from a course based primarily on practical workshops and group discussion, but will benefit more from private study and lectures. The use of some participative methods would broaden their experience, but should not be relied upon entirely if you want them to come to grips with the subject matter. Conversely, your 'experiencer' will be bored with chalk/talk and book learning, and learn best from doing things and discussing them with others. To get the most out of off-the-job training it is important therefore to know both your staff and the course methods.

A final thought on learning preferences – organisations also develop learning styles as part of their culture. Does your organisation 'do it now, faster', and leave little time for review and planning, or does it spend so long considering and reflecting that decisions are rarely made before they are out of date? To learn is to change; it is both a pain and a pleasure.

Resources
There is a lot of material written on learning styles, much of it theoretical and rather heavy to read. The following original texts are both readable and practical. *Organisational Psychology*, David A. Kolb, Rubin M. Irwin and James M. McIntyre (Prentice Hall, 1984). *Manual of Learning Styles*, Peter Honey and Alan Mumford (Honey, 1982).

5

Communicate Effectively

You may remember the old army story used in training new recruits in the skills of signalling and communications. The commanding officer at brigade headquarters turned a dangerous shade of puce when he received a signal from a unit in the field of action which read, 'Send three and fourpence. We are going to a dance'. The message which had actually been sent from the field was 'Send reinforcements. We are going to advance'. The meaning (if not the wish) had been distorted somewhere along the numerous lines of communication.

There are obvious sources of interference to communication when there are various physical and technological barriers between sender and receiver, including audibility, legibility, technical and human error in transcription or translation. Some of these may be outside our direct control. But it is too easy to blame the medium or the recipient for not understanding what we mean.

The basis of good communication is to think ourselves into the position of the person receiving the message, and thereby accept our share of responsibility for their understanding.

A middle manager in the public sector complained that in one area of his work he could not improve his performance because other people did not co-operate. The work included a series of consultations which had to take place with various organisations and members of the public before the next stage of a predetermined process could be achieved. Work was always behind schedule, and complaints were made that everything took too long. The consultation had to be carried out in writing, and the manager said that he got letters out quickly but some people did not bother to reply, and there was therefore nothing he could do about it. When we examined these letters, I was surprised he got any replies at all. They were written in the kind of 'gobbledegook' that only public officials seem able to invent. There was little indication of urgency or any incentive identified as to why the recipient should reply. After a little soul searching the manager realised that his unit did have some responsibility for ensuring that its letters were understood as well as being out on time. He also instituted a 'chase-up' system by correspondence and telephone, which broadened the role of his clerical staff and gave them a new challenge.

When what we want out of the communication is more important to us than to the person we are dealing with, it is essential to make sure they understand our intentions, and not just to assume they have the same interest in our goals that we have. When an English tourist was driving through Scotland, he became confused at a crossroads where the signpost indicated the road to Forfar in two opposite directions. He saw a local inhabitant thinning turnips in a field and called out to him, 'Does it matter which road I take to Forfar?' The reply he got was, 'Not tae me it doesne!'

These barriers affect communication between the various parts of an organisation as well as externally to customers and suppliers, but you may think that in face-to-face contact with your own team, this is not a problem. Anyway, communication is one of those things we like to feel we are rather good at – it all sounds pretty lucid from our side of the conversation. If the other chap is too thick or doesn't listen, its hardly our fault – or is it?

Even when you are standing three feet away from someone, there are numerous sources of interference which can prevent the message you wish to convey being received with the same meaning by the person you are talking to. For example:

- your ability to express yourself, including the choice of words as well as speed and tone of voice

- the other person's ability:
    - both to hear and to listen
    - level of comprehension of the words and concepts you use
    - feelings, about you, about the subject, and about themselves and life in general
    - attitude towards you, the subject, themselves and the world generally.

Of course, with two-way communication, the number of barriers is doubled because you each have to get through these layers of potential interference to reach the other. To understand and find ways through the barriers are vital to staff development because clear two-way communication is not only the foundations of a good working relationship, it is the key to all the other means of development – giving and receiving feedback, coaching, instructing, counselling and appraising. Good management depends on effective transactions between people, and within our own team it is often the verbal ones that are the most important.

Feelings and attitudes are difficult barriers to overcome, but if we understand them, and put ourselves in the other person's place, the messages we send have a good chance of being understood in the way we want them to be.

Eric Berne invented a simple framework for analysing personal transactions which helps us to recognise the frame of reference from which we are speaking, and from which the other person is receiving, and explains why communications so often get crossed. He called it Transactional Analysis, and the concept was so well received that his book, *Games People Play*, became a bestseller.

Berne recognised that people's behaviour can change from one situation to another. We can be playful at times, aloof or bossy at other times. Someone who throws his weight around at work may be a 'cuddly puppy' at home. Sometimes our response depends on whom we are with, or how they have approached us, or it may be simply the state of mind we are in at the time.

Such changes in mood are indicated by what we say to people, and especially how we say it – tone of voice, facial expressions and other non-verbal gestures. Berne identified a pattern in these states of mind, or 'ego states', as he called them. He believed there are three basic ego states, each with their characteristic behaviour, which we move into and out of in response to what is going on around us. He described them as follows:

1. **Parent** – this ego state reflects the actions and values of our parents and their behaviour towards us throughout our lives, including attitudes to right and wrong. We learn the words and actions of being 'parental' from watching our parents, including the authoritarian expressions such as 'Don't', frowning and finger-pointing of the critical parent, as well as expressions of concern such as 'It'll be all right', soothing tones and the comforting physical contact of the caring parent.

2. **Child** – in the child ego state, we experience the feelings and emotions of our childhood. As with the parent state, there are two variants. First, there is the free child – unrestrained, fun-loving, emotional, creative. In this state we can giggle, tease, day-dream, and throw tantrums. Second, there is the adapted child – conditioned by parental control to manipulate in order to gain reward or avoid punishment. In this state, we express dependency ('You do it for me'), fear, appealing to others, and uncritical compliance.

3. **Adult** – the characteristics of the adult ego state are associated with the learning we achieve when we grow up, and include the use of rational thought and factual analysis in problem-solving and other transactions. It is the state in which we learn and practise new skills, and develop our own aptitudes and abilities. It is therefore a particularly important ego state to recognise, use and encourage during staff development activities.

The following are the key principles to remember in applying this to your role as the boss:

- The essence of each ego state is as follows: parent (attitudes/ opinions), child (feelings/emotions), adult (thoughts/learning).
- They are all normal and essential to a balanced life; no one is 'good' or 'bad'.
- Each of us is in one ego state or the other at any given time, and will initiate, or react to, behaviour accordingly.
- The ego state we choose to use in any situation will provoke or encourage the ego state from which the other person responds.

When the ego states used are complementary, the communication is usually understood and accepted by both parties. For example:

- Boss tells subordinate off in a cross, finger-wagging way (critical parent), and subordinate accepts being treated as naughty child and either submits apologetically (adapted child), or gives a flippant response (free child).

- Boss looks pleadingly at secretary and says what an awful meeting he's had (adapted child), secretary stops what she is doing and makes coffee (caring parent).

- Boss shares joke about tricky work situation and fantasises about getting rid of the board (free child); subordinate responds with a few fantasies of his own on the same theme (free child). The same 'free child' match would exist if both gave free reign to creative ideas without fear of having them criticised or ridiculed by the other.

Where things go wrong is when the lines get crossed, i.e. the role you have imposed upon the other person by the ego state you have chosen to use is not accepted by them:

- Boss to subordinate having difficulty with a task, 'Don't worry, give it to me and I'll do it for you' (caring parent); subordinate responds, 'Don't take over, you should let me do things myself' (critical parent). The 'child' role has been rejected and if the boss now also retaliates with critical parent, 'Don't you speak to me like that', a row is brewing and communication has ceased to be effective.

- Boss rushes back from important meeting. 'The MD needs these budget figures up-dated for tomorrow; do you have the necessary information to do that?' (adult); subordinate responds, 'Why do I always have to do these last minute jobs?' (either free child or adapted child, depending on whether the tone is rebellious or wheedling). The subordinate has refused to accept the responsibility of an adult ego state, and tries to engage the boss's 'parent', to save him from the unwanted task. Alternatively, the subordinate may encourage the boss to share the 'child' state in response to the MD seen as 'critical parent'.

It is clear from these examples that although all ego states are equally acceptable forms of behaviour in themselves, communication becomes ineffective when they are used in inappropriate situations, or when the ego states adopted by each party do not complement each other. Being able to analyse transactions in this way is helpful in maintaining good relationships, which depend on effective communication and mutual understanding. It enables you to adjust your approach where necessary to prevent lines of communication being crossed, to understand why the other person is responding in a particular way, and to prevent yourself being drawn by others into ego states which are not appropriate for the task in hand.

But there is a much more important application for staff development. As I mentioned at the beginning of this chapter, it is in the 'adult' state we do our thinking, analysing, problem-solving and learning. In any situation where you wish to train and develop staff, it is therefore essential that you adopt the adult ego state, and encourage your subordinate to do the same. If your approach to appraisal, coaching or giving feedback is that of the caring parent who saves subordinates from difficult tasks and protects them from making mistakes, or is that of the critical parent who is judgmental and authoritarian, the responses you are likely to get are those of the child state – compliance to exactly what you say rather than their thinking for themselves, or rebellion. Neither leads to learning or development. If instead you get retaliation from the parent state, it is likely to damage the relationship as well. The following are some of the characteristics of the adult ego state which you can use to make communication effective for staff development:

- Avoid expressions of emotion: anger, sorrow, anxiety.
- Use questioning techniques to provoke thought and analysis rather than telling people what do do.
- Encourage pride in learning and achieving as a reward in itself rather than using sticks and carrots as incentives to learn; they might increase output in the short term, but they don't create learning.
- Use realistic assessments and stick to the facts rather than make general criticisms or judgements.
- Don't smother; work out the level of risk you are prepared to take, and after appropriate training and guidance, let subordinates make mistakes and learn from them.
- Accept assertive behaviour from subordinates and be prepared to discuss problems on an equal footing, and as a joint activity.
- Use a calm and even tone of voice, regular eye contact, and facial/body movements of openness and acceptance.
- Listen, evaluate, and be constructive in your responses.

Standing outside a theatre one night, I overheard a snippet of conversation as a couple were getting out of a taxi. The woman was saying, 'It's so hard to behave like a lady when you don't behave like a gentleman.. .' If everyone else doesn't know about parent, child and adult states or, worse still, does, and prefers to play their own games, how can you operate in the ego state which is most suitable for you and for the task in hand? More importantly, how can you establish an adult state on both sides when training or developing staff?

The answer depends to some extent on the situation and the people concerned. Refusing to be manipulated into responding in ways you would prefer not to, by calmly and staunchly sticking to the adult state in what you say and the way that you say it, usually works, although it may take a little patience and practice. If appropriate, you can stop the 'game' by being completely open in discussing what is taking place and the stances you are both taking in relation to what it is you are both trying to achieve – done with the behaviour characteristic of the adult state of course, for if you behave like a 'critical parent', you have been hooked into the other person's game!

If there is insufficient mutual trust, or the risks are too great for this kind of openness, using your adult state to re-establish shared goals will often encourage the other party to respond from his or her adult state. If a situation has become a little tense, temporary use of the playful behaviour of the free child may give you both a breathing space, and reduce any perceived threat, thus enabling you to revert to adult in a calmer atmosphere, which should encourage the other person to do the same. (Avoid any other quick switch though, as this is likely to lead to confusion and mistrust.)

Like lots of learning, it can be fun understanding and recognising the ego states from which other people's behaviour originates. To familiarise yourself with the idea, do a little people watching, at meetings, in other offices, shops, and in your own department. When the outcome is important to you, consciously work out the appropriate state from which to work and the behaviour that will entail. Share the knowledge with your subordinates – communication is one area where you definitely don't gain by keeping the means of effectiveness to yourself.

Resources

For a full treatment of Transactional Analysis, see *Games People Play*, E. Berne's original book (Penguin, 1968).

6

Induct New Recruits

Some managers select and run in a new car with more care and consideration than a new employee. They take the attitude that new people should be left to sink or swim. Apart from the loss of production and turnover costs resulting from those who sink, there can be longer term detrimental effects upon the whole team by those who choose to float. Having discovered they are in the wrong job or the wrong organisation, and unable to afford to cut their losses, they decide to hang on and ride until something else comes along. These are the marginal employees, demotivated, performing under par, a deadweight on the team but still on the payroll.

The process of developing people begins the day they arrive, and it is not just school-leavers and junior grades who need good induction. Middle and senior managers, and production, technical and administrative staff need to be introduced quickly and effectively into the work and culture of your team. The sooner it becomes their team too, the sooner they will want to contribute to its output. The same goes for transfers from other departments or companies in the same group. Those people transferred may have served for some time in the company and be generally familiar with company policy, but they will not be your people, sharing your values, unless you take care to nurture them in their new roles.

Induction sets the pattern for longer term motivation, commitment and loyalty. It influences the range and quality of relationships new employees make within and across departments. The lasting impact of early relationships and information should never be underestimated. We are all social animals and soon learn from birth what is acceptable behaviour in various situations and such groups as the family, school, clubs and our own peer group. We do this by gradually absorbing the prevailing attitudes and values around us. This same process of socialisation is equally powerful at work, but to leave induction to the natural process not only unnecessarily prolongs the exercise, it can result in the wrong attitudes and values being passed on. If the boss does not make time to share his vision with the new recruit, the least committed members of the workforce soon will!

Induction really begins with recruitment advertising. It is at this stage that potential candidates begin to create their own fantasies about the job and the organisation. The way selection is carried out, and subsequent documentation and recruitment procedures will either enhance the fantasy or begin to turn the dream into a nightmare. If you want to develop your staff well for the future by starting at the beginning, then recruitment is too important to leave to the personnel department. Have your say in drafting the advertisement, and in selection and interview procedures.

Once the choice has been made, take a personal interest in the appointees' circumstances, family relocation problems, removal expenses and timing of the start date. Be seen by the new recruit and your team to be doing everything you can to ensure a smooth entry into the organisation. This partnership approach to recruitment may be a new experience for some personnel officers, but it is worth the effort of establishing your right to participate fully, and you will reap benefits in the long term. There may be a gap of weeks or even a couple of months before the new recruit starts work, a hiatus between two loyalties and two environments that can be a time of uncertainty and doubt.

The enthusiasm and commitment following a successful appointment needs to be maintained by putting the new person in immediate contact with his or her new boss, sending background information on the company, e.g. back numbers of the house journal or departmental newsletter, and providing advance information on the new job. Arrangements should also be made for the new recruits to spend a couple of days familiarising themselves with the new environment before the official start date. If people are moving in from another part of the country, delegate to someone the task of sending them local newspapers until they arrive in the area.

Rather than let the grapevine do its inevitable worst, give relevant information to the rest of your subordinates on the new person and his or her role in the group. Better still, adopt the practice of peer group interviewing whenever the post demands team/project work, or when close liaison with colleagues is essential to the success of the task.

Attention to detail and investment of time at this stage will be repaid tenfold when your new recruit arrives with an image of an organisation and a boss he really wants to work for from day one. What happens next depends on your organisation's training and recruitment policy. One major car manufacturer does not allow any new recruit near a company desk or workbench for 8 weeks. During this time, new personnel go through an intensive induction course covering technical and administrative procedures and, of course, company culture and values.

Public sector employers tend to do far less and a 1-day general induction course sometime during the first 2 months of employment, and perhaps a wordy and largely incomprehensible handbook, may be all that is provided.

If your organisation has a formal induction course, ensure that you know exactly what takes place and brief new staff on its purpose and content before they attend. If possible, offer to make a short presentation at the course, or join the group informally at the coffee or lunch break. If handled properly, such a show of interest is usually welcomed by trainers. It demonstrates commitment to your own staff as well as keeping in close touch with their early experiences. Once you know what is going on, you may wish to make some constructive suggestions for developing or improving the induction course. You have a genuine vested interest; it is your people who are attending it. If you are the managing director or chief executive of the company, you should in any case be playing a key role in both the formal and informal aspects of company induction courses.

The existence of formal courses does not absolve the manager from responsibility for initial workplace induction. During the first few weeks and months of a new job there is a great deal to learn, technically and socially. Planning this learning process systematically will ensure the early effectiveness of new people. Ask new starters to arrive on their first day an hour or so after the working day has begun. This enables you do deal with any urgent matters before devoting time exclusively to the new member of your team.

There should be an initial welcome and briefing to clarify any outstanding recruitment or personal problems. If there are any, take action immediately. If your new recruit has just been gazumped and has his wife, mother-in-law, two kids and the dog living in a caravan in the company car park, his mind will not be entirely on his new job.

Unless recruitment is frequent, it is easy to forget all the information that needs to be covered. A formal checklist, which new recruit and supervisor can work through together, is useful, especially if there is space on the form for some basic data to be written in and retained by the new recruit as an aide-mémoire. The following could be used as a basis for drawing up your own checklist:

- Desk, workstation, tools, equipment or any information necessary to do the job should be ready and working.
- The new starter's immediate supervisor should have the clear responsibility and time to introduce him or her to the job, which may demand daily briefings over the first few weeks.
- A clear explanation of the team's objectives, the standards of work expected, and how they are measured.
- An outline of the unwritten rules and informal networks in the section and department.
- A tour of the premises and staff facilities, and introduction to colleagues, support staff, subordinates, and such other key personnel as the janitor and the chief executive.
- Health and safety procedures and any special requirements of their section.

- Details of who in the organisation can answer which kind of query, both work and personal.
- Conditions of service, including training and promotion prospects.
- Departmental structures and objectives and their relation to the work of the new employee. (In due course, the same for the company as a whole.)

Putting all this information across needs to be paced and reconfirmed at appropriate times. A brief and well laid out handbook on your own section or department can be useful for new people to refer to. Don't write it yourself. Develop one of your subordinates by delegating the task to him or her, preferably the one who joined the team most recently and can still remember the things newcomers most needed to know when they first started. A barrage of information and new faces on the first day is likely to cause acute mental indigestion.

If the new person is your immediate subordinate, you will be doing most of these briefings yourself. If not, you will need to monitor how the induction is progressing.

New employees often think that to ask a lot of questions, particularly of the boss, will make them appear incompetent. But it is always better to enable them to ask questions and get answers rather than leave them in uncertainty.

The system of sponsorship is a useful way of encouraging this. Select someone on the same grade and preferably doing similar work but with whom the new person will not be working in competition. Brief the sponsor on the role, which is to act as a 'workmate', answer questions, give friendly guidance and generally ease the new person into the environment. Sponsors also provide an initial social contact and act as a valuable link to the informal networks and mores of the workplace. But remember the power of socialisation and select sponsors with care. The recognition you give to the sponsors by placing in them your trust and confidence will also be a powerful motivator and so will the way you handle induction. It demonstrates not only how well you value a new employee but is also seen as a reflection of how you feel about the other people who work for you. In nine times out of ten, they will meet your expectations of them, and match your loyalty and consideration with theirs.

Resources

ACAS (Advisory, Conciliation and Arbitration Service) produces a good series of booklets on staffing matters and associated legislation, including one on induction. The Industrial Society also produces its own booklet, *Induction*.

7

Pay Attention to Your Staff

When did you last pay your secretary a personal compliment, or pass the receptionist with more than a nod and a grunt?

None of us likes to be taken for granted, as so much office furniture, and the results of paying a little attention with a brief word of recognition or concern to all the people for whom you have any responsibility, and even those you don't, are well worth the effort.

We all have a need to have our existence registered by others – several times a day. It is part of being social animals. Those who work in open-plan offices, in groups or in jobs where they move around and meet people have a greater chance of getting the amount of personal feedback they need than those who don't.

Psychologists call it 'stroking'. The amount of strokes needed to maintain a sense of well-being varies with individuals: some need a lot, others can get by with much less. The most powerful are positive strokes – words and looks of praise and pleasure. But so great is the need for recognition, that even negative strokes are better than none at all! Without them people can lose confidence, feel out of things, devalued, and may then withdraw their commitment. If they don't get sufficient strokes from you, they may spend time 'social-visiting' around the office to get their strokes elsewhere. From your point of view, regular attention to your staff confirms your presence as a leader; it is difficult to be loyal to an absentee landlord. From their point of view, it demonstrates a caring boss and a caring organisation. If your business is caring for customers and clients, and you want to instil this value in your subordinates, the most effective way to do so is by example.

Strokes and values cannot be transmitted by memoranda. It takes face-to-face contact. One young chief executive, taking up his post in a local authority, stopped the practice of memos being sent to heads of departments, and instructed them never to send memos to him. He believed that effective communication between boss and immediate subordinate had to be face-to-face. It also enables the boss to give regular strokes.

Receiving regular personal recognition increases loyalty, and the wish to respond by fulfilling your expectations. Feedback on performance, both good and bad, is accepted and acted upon more readily. You are seen as a human being and approachable, rather than someone from whom errors and problems should be hidden – until they grow so big that you can't help tripping over them yourself.

A boss I once had used to send cards when his staff were off sick, and visit longer term cases. On one occasion my husband was taken ill suddenly while I was abroad on a work assignment, and my boss visited him in hospital. As a manager he was no 'soft touch': where results were concerned he was as hard as nails. But he knew the value of caring and being seen to care for his people, and it took him to the top.

If you create an ambience of caring, all your staff will feel the reflection of it even when they themselves are not personally on the receiving end.

Caring need not be restricted to your immediate subordinates. When a long-standing office cleaner was due for her retirement presentation, the head of department where she cleaned not only insisted on giving the presentation himself, but went down to her storeroom to bring her up to the office because he was told she had 'got nerves' over the event. Such actions create the image of a leader worth making every effort for, and their impact is long lasting.

Practise MBWA – management by walking about – and you will have ample opportunities to administer strokes. It need only take a minute. Ask about a recent holiday, comment on a new outfit, car, or appointment to a local committee. Enquire about a new baby, school progress, or a spouse's new job. Keep a small notebook and record any useful bits of information. Refer to it before meeting anyone you have recently seen. Once you make a habit of it, you will have a fund of background information on which to base future brief but caring comments which say 'I value you' in a simple, practical and acceptable way. The caring has to be genuine of course. If you really don't care that much about people, perhaps you should become a lighthouse keeper?

8

Delegate for Development

At a weekend residential course, a group of junior and middle managers were attending a workshop on delegation. They came from a wide range of backgrounds – heavy industry, public utilities, electronics, insurance, local government and manufacturing. As a warm-up session, they were asked to describe from their own experience what delegation meant to them. Here are some of their responses:

- 'I get the boring and dirty jobs my boss doesn't like doing.'
- 'When I was given a really interesting assignment that was in my speciality, the boss was on my back the whole time telling me how to do it. I didn't really get a chance to get my teeth into it.'
- 'Every so often I get a heap of papers through the internal mail, mostly routine returns and requests which have sat on my supervisor's desk until he's noticed the deadline is long overdue and somebody had better do something about it – that's usually me, and I'm on a hiding to nothing before I even start.'
- 'I don't know – the boss keeps everything to herself. I don't even know what she does most of the time.'

The biggest work problem these people had was the boss. The sad thing is that the work overload and low morale cascade down the organisation like an avalanche, crushing the poor blighters at the bottom. At each level, people have little scope to do anything other than pass it down the line along with their resentment. Proper delegation is the keystone of effective management. There are good reasons why this should be so and like most good reasons they include a lot of self-interest:

- It gives you time to do work only you can or should do, and lets you concentrate on priorities of your own, like thinking, keeping two steps ahead of the game, and looking down to see what you're about to step into.

● It frees you to move about your patch, to network through the organisation, and to demonstrate your availability for promotion.

● It increases the pool of knowledge and experience in the team and builds your reputation for having good people, which attracts other good people.

● It optimises the use you make of each of your subordinates' skills and initiative, and gives you a chance to assess their promotion potential.

● It demonstrates trust in your staff and recognition of their worth. Both are prized rewards and powerful motivators.

● It develops in them new skills, greater confidence, and better understanding of what you are trying to achieve.

Delegation is not an optional extra: it is the only way to run an effective organisation. But there are ways of doing it which, while not detracting from the other benefits, maximise the developmental aspects for your subordinates.

Delegating a task or function does not absolve you from responsibility for the outcome. You don't give your responsibility away, but you do have to share your power to enable the delegatee to operate effectively. You lend it out, and if you want it maintained in good order, you must exercise sound judgement as to what each person can achieve and how much training, preparation and supervision are needed in each instance.

The quality of your judgement will depend on how well you know your team. Make sure you really know who you are dealing with before embarking on wholesale delegation. If necessary, spend extra time with them first, just to get to know them and their capabilities and aspirations better.

Define the task you are delegating, the powers which may be exercised in doing it, the standards you expect, the outcome required, and when and how you want them to report to you during and on completion of the task. Do you really want them to come to you 'any time you have a problem?' If you are managing your time effectively, you will want to limit your availability within reason.

Tell them what results you want, why, by when, and where (if necessary), but leave them to work on the how. They may have better ideas on this than you have.

Give a complete task in which they can feel a sense of achievement, rather than making them a 'gofer' on some menial element of a more interesting assignment. A complex project may be broken up into smaller but nonetheless useful and stimulating tasks which someone can get their teeth into.

You may not be delegating a task as such, but your role as the boss – during annual leave, for example. (If you don't take leave, you should. How car people grow if you're always around the place?) Give them experience at trying out the role for short periods of time first.

Whoever you are grooming to stand in for you, take them along to a significant meeting which you normally chair or in which you play a major role. Brief them beforehand on the background and your expectations, and review with them the outcome afterwards – what happened and why. When the next meeting is due, deliberately absent yourself. Brief your stand-in on both the best outcome and the bottom line, but leave him or her to work out how to get it. If you don't want both of you to look silly, define the power and responsibility he or she can use and make it as much as possible. There is no point in giving them the experience if they are going to be bound and gagged, and it won't achieve your objectives anyway. Debrief them as soon after the meeting as possible, giving both praise and constructive feedback. If appropriate, let them follow through subsequent action.

If you do this a few times with different aspects of your role, not only do you increase the security of your operations by having someone you know you can depend on when necessary, but the briefings and coaching can clarify your role and objectives in your own mind.

When you do go on leave, give your stand-in as much freedom of action as possible, and let him or her use your office. The symbols of authority will increase self-confidence and help the individual to operate better in relation to other people.

When lending your responsibility for this, or any delegation, it is essential not only to define the extent of the responsibility, but to tell everyone else. If you're making Janet responsible for the car-leasing scheme, send a memo to anyone who should know and tell them so. If someone phones you about the scheme, pass them to Janet. Don't pull the rug from under her feet by meddling in the job yourself, even if the caller is a pal of yours!

Develop leadership skills by delegating a complete project to a group, but give the responsibility for sub-delegating the parts, and for reporting back to you, to a nominated member of the group. Make sure the group is clear about its leader's role and powers, but let the leader do the briefing on the project. If it is the first leadership responsibility for your nominee, it may take him or her a little while to establish authority.

Your best course of action is watchful neglect. Be available for the group leader to discuss problems with you, but don't dent the leader's vulnerable position by taking over or issuing orders direct to group members, even difficult ones. You selected the leader, so demonstrate faith in your own judgement and work through him or her.

It is important to specify the standards required of a delegated task, but this does not mean that it has to be done just the way you would do it. If correspondence or report writing is delegated, it is demoralising to have everything rewritten just because the boss's favourite phrases are not used. If the objectives are achieved on schedule, then that is all that is required. If they are not, then either you have selected the wrong task for the wrong person, or more training and preparation are necessary. If the former, reassess your knowledge of the person and the task, and achieve a better match next time. If the latter, give more coaching. But remember that delegation includes the right to make the wrong decision and learn from the experience.

Weighing up the risks is your responsibility before you decide to delegate. Increasing the level of supervision is not a good solution. You must identify a task which the person can do after adequate briefing but with the minimum of supervision. This does not mean there is no need to monitor. You can't dump the job and forget it, but you don't want to spend your time breathing down someone's neck: they won't like it either. That is not delegation. People also need adequate resources to do the job. This includes a realistic amount of time, bearing in mind their total workload.

If you have left something on your desk until the deadline for action has expired – handle it yourself. Don't delegate work because you find it tedious or distasteful. Constantly evaluate during each day, whether it is absolutely essential that only you do this task. If not, decide to whom you could delegate it, and plan at the outset how it will develop that person. Delegate tasks you enjoy; your enthusiasm will be contagious.

Some people have more confidence than others in taking on new or bigger tasks and you may have to develop them gradually and know when they have reached their limits. At that stage, don't try to stretch them further but concentrate instead on variety and interest in the work allocated to them. This will maintain their momentum and motivation. Everybody, including the office junior-cum-teamaker has potential which can be tapped by delegating additional responsibility if you get to know them well enough. People are always full of surprises.

If delegation is to develop people as well as get the job done, feedback and reward for success are essential. Feedback must be immediate, specific and genuine, and should include constructive suggestions, praise and encouragement. A sense of achievement and recognition are rewards prized by most people. If it can be accompanied by material gain, then that is a bonus, but it is not essential to the development process.

The spin-off for you is that learning to delegate well forces you to define your priorities, objectives, and standards before you can brief anyone else on them. Managers who don't delegate don't usually know where they are going.

Resources

Although delegation appears somewhere in most management books, there is little written about it as a subject in itself. The best resource is to discuss it with other managers whose work you admire.

9

Coach

You may be among the minority of good managers who are natural coaches. They coach their staff all the time as their normal style of working and barely know they are doing it. But many do not. The usual excuse is lack of time, but the real reason is often that they have never done it, don't know quite where to start, and prefer to dodge the issue than take up the challenge. Like much staff development, the results are often long term and not always easy to quantify, but if you talk to any managers who consistently coach subordinates, they will tell you that the pay-off is worth the effort.

Some people get very caught up in defining what coaching is as distinct from teaching, training, delegating, counselling or giving feedback. As in any development activity, it is more effective to do it than to worry about defining it. The main objective can be lost by getting hooked on categories. When one of the great jazz singers, Big Bill Broonzie, was challenged that some of his songs were not real folk songs, he replied, 'It's all folk song. I ain't never heard a horse sing!' It's all staff development, and while all the activities mentioned above may come into coaching at one time or another, the important thing is to be aware of the main purpose of coaching and use whatever skills and processes you find helpful.

If achieving an objective through the effective use of resources is a manager's role, then coaching is an essential part of that role, because human resources are among the most crucial and most expensive, and are rarely used to their full potential. The purpose of coaching is to increase and improve the performance of individuals by helping them to develop the attitudes and skills appropriate to their current tasks while they are achieving them. It is to do with the practicalities of each day, and is how most of us learn most of what we know.

The emphasis is on 'helping' rather than simply telling people what to do, giving them the answers, or criticising their performance. It is about guiding them through the steps of asking themselves the right questions about what they are doing, enabling them to find the information they need, and then allowing them to make the decision or take the action. This way they remain in control of the learning, and it becomes self-sustaining, i.e. they can apply both the learning process, and the work principles they have discovered, to other situations, and do it successfully even when you are not standing at their shoulder.

It amounts to enabling people to learn without creating dependency and is one of the most difficult things to do well – no less so for professional teachers and trainers, who often get their ego-trips from being 'the one who knows'. This is counterproductive for them, as well as their pupils. But even more so for you. Trainers only have their students for the duration of the course; you have your subordinates all the time, and if they only perform well when you are telling them what to do, you won't have much time left for anything else.

The manager who is a puppet master is as tied by the strings as his puppets. It means that you need the courage to let subordinates make mistakes. They can be a powerful force for learning, which rescue would not. People will make mistakes anyway; at least when coaching you can decide what risks you are prepared to take and to what extent you can, or wish to, control the outcome. But don't leave them exposed if things do go wrong.

Coaching is not an occasion to pull rank. Managers who are so lacking in self-confidence that they have to display their authority like a shield carried between themselves and their subordinates need some coaching themselves before trying to give it to others. A good coach creates a feeling of partnership and mutual frankness. Success depends to a large extent on the quality of the underlying boss-subordinate relationship. If this is good, and staff development is part of your management style, coaching will be easier and more rewarding for you both.

It takes a lot of time, but there may be another cost too. When you coach, you are automatically passing on and reinforcing the values on which your work is based. This is an extremely important benefit to you and the organisation, but it exposes your own belief in those values and the extent to which you live them.

The major benefits of coaching apply to any grade of employee and include:

- providing training/development through carrying out the tasks for which training is being given
- improving quality/quantity of performance by developing appropriate skills, values and attitudes ~which can be applied immediately
- stretching the ability of subordinates to achieve higher level of work
- enabling subordinates to learn from experience, and to continue the learning process independently
- encouraging better problem-solving techniques and solutions
- increasing motivation and commitment.

Coaching can be used to help a subordinate over a difficult work problem, or as a remedial activity in cases of poor performance. It turns a problem into a learning situation. In fact, a coaching plan should form the final stage of a formal appraisal interview, drawn up jointly between employee and senior. But coaching should not be limited only to dealing with difficulties in a reactive way. It should be used pro-actively for positive development.

When your subordinate has a 'first' coming up – first solo sales trip, public presentation, supervisory post, negotiating meeting, night duty, or promotion interview – it is an ideal occasion for some coaching before and after the event.

Coach during a particularly challenging or interesting assignment, when new skills are needed, or when you are doing a task others could learn from.

New employees should be coached during their first few months. It is not just a fair-weather activity either. Working through a crisis is an ideal opportunity to develop capacity for thinking and coping under pressure.

The whole point of coaching is to use real work challenges as the medium for learning. What better than a real live crisis in which to learn crisis management – in its best sense of course. In short, a good coach recognises when something can be learned from the daily round of work and ensures his or her subordinates gain by learning it.

Before embarking on coaching for the first time, here are a few things you need to check out:

- Make sure you know the work well enough. If you don't, another member of the team may, and there is no reason why colleagues should not coach each other – it's a good team-building skill to develop (and another opportunity for coaching!).

- Ensure that the targets you set can be seen by the subordinate as achievable; preferably set them as a joint exercise. The subordinate must also be able to assess his or her own progress and know when he or she has achieved the target. So should all your staff.

- The subordinate should be able to use the skills and approaches directly in his or her current work, not at some vague time in the future.

- Assess whether you know the subordinate well enough to judge the right kind of approach. If subordinates have not been used to training, or have a chip on their shoulder, they may be resistant to the idea at first. Coaching is not something you do *to* people, but a joint activity that requires their full commitment. Older employees in particular may need to be handled with considerable tact when they are launched into their first coaching session, and progress may be slow initially.

Once you have decided to coach, and have identified the opportunity and the person, you are ready to think through how you actually do it. The personal skills you will need are the ability to listen rather than tell, and a great deal of patience.

Allow yourself sufficient time with the minimum of interruptions, especially when starting coaching with someone for the first time. Their place is better than yours, unless there is too much noise and interference. Adopt a questioning approach, not the third degree, but as a means of showing them how to ask questions of themselves which make them think more deeply about what they are doing and why, about alternative courses of action and their implications.

Avoid saying, 'What you ought to do is…', for at that point they will stop thinking for themselves, and stop learning too. Instead ask 'What if…' questions.

Good coaching actually teaches people how to learn. For example, if the learning opportunity is a new experience they are about to have, like negotiating a new contract, ask them how they intend to approach the situation. Encourage them to question their tactics and think about their implications. Act as a sounding board and play devil's advocate to stimulate further thinking around the problem. Draw them out and encourage promising responses, giving them facts and information only when necessary (not to show how much you know). You might suggest they go and talk to somebody else who has some special knowledge which is relevant, indicate other sources of information, or suggest the sort of things that might happen during the negotiation which they should consider.

End the session on an encouraging note, and agree on the appropriate stages for subsequent coaching and feedback on progress. When a decision has to be made, let the subordinate make it and learn from his or her experience afterwards. You will have to balance the results you want against the the value of the learning opportunity, but if you gave them the job in the first place, and have coached them effectively, you must exercise sufficient faith to give them authority to implement their decision.

Coaching for longer term projects uses the same approach but may consist of shorter, more frequent sessions mixed with feedback. For example, if your subordinates are preparing a budget, or working on design drawings, the coaching may consist of a few brief minutes asking pertinent questions and enlarging on alternatives which they can consider. If they decide to follow one of these up, you may then spend half an hour going over that particular aspect with them.

In coaching for technical skills you may need to provide the means of experimenting with ideas under controlled situations through which they learn for themselves how to develop workable techniques. This is more effective than simply telling them. What works for you may not work so well for them anyway.

Share your own relevant experiences with your subordinates. For example, if you are coaching for selection interview skills, let them sit in on an interview with you. Explain to them beforehand how you are preparing for it, what you want to come out of it, and go over with them afterwards what happened and why. You may have to be big enough to share some of your own mistakes, but there is no harm in demonstrating that even the boss knows how to learn from experience.

Reflect upon your past work when coaching subordinates to demonstrate ideas and approaches, but not as a blueprint for them to follow. Get them to reflect upon their own experience as it develops, and to draw conclusions from it which will help them with the next stage of the task.

Listen, encourage and stimulate. It takes time to develop coaching skills, but the more you do it, the easier it becomes. Review each coaching session and ask yourself some key questions. Did I really discuss, or was I selling my own ideas with no intention of changing them? Did I draw out all he or she could contribute at this stage, or did I miss some uncertain hints that I should have picked up and developed? Have I left him or her knowing what is expected next and inspired to do it?

In helping others to learn, you develop your own learning skills. Coaching others also helps you to question your own priorities and objectives in answering questions from your subordinates.

With sufficient practice, it becomes second nature to take advantage of learning opportunities in your subordinates' work and in your own, and to ensure that they learn and develop from both. After a while it becomes a way of life and you don't notice the effort, only the results.

10

Give Credit

Can you remember when you were an aspiring young professional, and all those brilliant reports you wrote for your boss? The faultless logic, the precision, the turn of phrase which you carefully polished – and how they were passed up through the organisation with your boss's name on them with barely a word of thanks to you, the author. There is nothing less geared to develop staff than to withhold, or worse still, purloin, their due credit for a job well done, whether it is a report, a good sales record, handling customers well, or maintaining the cleanest office in the building. There are many people who have had their work filched and then circulated over someone else's name on the grounds that 'it was done for the department' or some such excuse – usually with the department head's name on it, mind you.

A simple but genuinely meant 'Thank you' can mean a lot. Not one muttered twenty times a day to all and sundry until it becomes meaningless, but said fully, with eye contact and a smile.

A letter of thanks for a particularly good piece of work shows a little more appreciation on your part, or even a bottle of wine for the team, or cakes for the tea-break during a trying but successful week for the typing pool. Time taken to give feedback on a task can make clear your recognition of someone's achievement as well as give guidance on future work.

Work too can be seen as a reward by giving more responsibility, more interesting assignments, letting someone take the chance of a trip away to visit a customer or supplier, or letting them attend the meeting at which there is always a particularly good lunch. But that is not enough.

Giving rewards and giving credit are not quite the same thing. Giving credit is a reward of a kind, in that it is the public recognition of achievement to which the achiever has a right, because it is his or her particular effort which has produced it. To withhold credit, or let somebody else have it, is far worse than simply not offering a reward. It is taking something away from a subordinate which is his or her due, i.e. recognition, and recognition is more powerful than money as a motivator, and a far greater stimulus for self-development. Recognition shares with other rewards certain pre-requisites before it can be effective in developing staff:

- Subordinates must know the end result they are expected to achieve.
- They must have the necessary resources/ability/authority/time with which to achieve it.
- They must be able to recognise when it has been achieved.
- Most important, their expectations of receiving the recognition for it must be high. They must believe that you will give them credit for their work, because you always do. Effort is expended in proportion to the expectation that the reward will be forthcoming.

This means dealing fairly and consistently in giving credit, not only to your immediate subordinates, but all the way down the line. It also means making it known. Tell others, your boss, the chief executive, the chairman, about a good piece of work or display of initiative. Let your subordinate's name be associated with it. Mention important achievements or winning ideas in the company journal or departmental newsletter. Have a weekly or monthly spot on the staff noticeboard, in the canteen, or outside the executive suite in the 'corridors of power', where the names of all those who have exceeded sales targets, clinched a big contract, thought up a new scheme, or in any other way achieved performances which deserve credit, can be given personal recognition.

The element of competitiveness will be a stimulus to other staff, provided it is open competition, i.e. it is possible for everyone to perform in a way that earns them credit for it.

Rather than rewarding only the person who gets the highest returns, give credit to everyone who achieves or goes beyond a specified and realistic target. That way, instead of only one 'winner' and a lot of 'losers' who stop bothering, it opens up the competition for anyone who wants to win.

Credit should be given not only for the high level work of middle and senior managers, but for creditable performances at every level. A note in the newsletter to thank your office cleaner, in public, for maintaining exceptionally high standards, is likely to sustain a pride in the work and a feeling of being part of the team. If the standards are not high, when did you last acknowledge his or her existence? Cleaners, night workers, and others who make their contribution to the organisation when most other people are not around, are in particular need of recognition for their work, and rarely get it.

A big American fast food chain has a training system for its counter staff which awards badges of different colours, and star ratings, for different levels of achievement in learning the job. They are worn on the front of their uniforms. Next time you go in for a burger, ask one of the assistants about the badge they are wearing; they will tell you with pride what their five gold stars mean.

Other firms adopt methods which are less public, but have formal recognition and can be used more publicly when required. For example, an international cosmetics firm issues its employees with training 'passports'. When a course of training is successfully completed, it is officially entered in their passport and signed by the managing director, who automatically sees not only their achievement but which managers are developing their staff and which are not.

A good system of giving credit combines the recognition of an individual at a personal level with some form of wider publicity. But be careful not to install a scheme which becomes so bureaucratic in its measurement of performance that the end product no longer relates to the individual. A teaching establishment engaged in distance learning has a system of written assessments of its correspondence tutors, copies of which go to the tutors and their boss. Random samples of assignments being returned to students are monitored by two senior staff, who comment on the quality of the tutor's feedback and marking, and give a grade from A to D. Once two consecutive assignments are graded C, the next are automatically graded B. One tutor discovered that, despite getting phrases like 'excellent teaching' on the written assessment, she never got a grade higher than a B, which all Cs got eventually anyway. She was still trying to get someone to explain what you had to do to get an A, when the new academic year started, and despite maintaining her standards, which were reflected in the written comments, because it was a new year the grade was the statutory starting grade of C. This system of demotivation was very effective – she resigned!

When giving credit, keep it personal, make it public, and do it often, and you too will get recognition, not only for developing good people but for being big enough to give them the credit for it.

11

Give Feedback

During the Second World War, a Japanese soldier was posted to a tiny Pacific island to observe and report on any unusual shipping movements. He performed his duties as best he could, although eventually the radio packed up. He was still there, attempting to keep watch, 5 years after peace was declared. No one thought to tell him the war was over. With no regular communication, they had forgotten him.

There are subordinates like that. Receiving no feedback from their bosses, they either grind away listlessly at tasks the relevance of which they no longer understand or care about, or they find substitute forms of interaction by becoming the office socialite – always off chatting to somebody else.

All of us need feedback at work and at home for normal healthy life. It is part of confirming our existence and creating our self-esteem. We believe in ourselves through other people's recognition of us and what we do. If we want to turn someone into a 'non-person', we do it by withholding all forms of feedback - 'sending them to Coventry' - and it can break the strongest character.

Feedback can be either positive or negative. It can be communicated verbally through words and sound or by non-verbal looks and gestures. The latter can have enormous impact, and as we give and receive feedback constantly in our social interactions, we often do so unwittingly and can give damaging negative messages if we are not aware of the process.

To develop staff, feedback should be given on their work performance and on the effect they have on other people around them. You make them aware of what they are doing and how they are doing it in such a way as to reinforce or create desirable behaviour with positive feedback and praise, and discourage undesired behaviour with negative feedback.

For effective development, the positive should exceed the negative. Negative feedback alone is better than none at all, but not a lot! For example, if one of your subordinates is technically competent but demonstrates favouritism in dealings with staff, give positive feedback on the competence by praising some recent piece of work, but point out that favouritism will cause trouble for him or her sometime in the future. The person may not be aware of this behaviour. If you have a good relationship with this individual, this brief negative feedback may be all that is required to create change. When the change does occur, give positive feedback to reinforce it.

Although feedback is essential in management for general welfare as well as to maintain motivation and improve performance, its significance in staff development is that it is an essential adjunct to learning. Experience alone may ensure no more than survival rather than development. At worst, things may be learned through experience which you do not want. Feedback creates the desire to learn and apply the things you positively encourage. It is therefore more than satisfying the need to know 'How am I doing?' or 'How am I being received by other people?' It is in itself the most effective way of learning and can take place at work as a continuous process with a boss who wants to develop his staff.

Like most worthwhile activities, it is not easy and requires courage, skill and mutual respect. Give feedback to everyone for whom you have responsibility. The amount and frequency will be greater for those reporting directly to you, but give it also to their subordinates all the way down the line – not as a way of interfering, but to give the recognition which all those under you will appreciate. It is the only reliable way to transfer and reinforce the values you want to permeate right through the organisation. This will be enhanced if, at the same time, you tell them about things that you are doing and, if you listen, you will get valuable feedback not only on other people's view of what is going on, but on yourself as well.

There are no rules about when feedback should be given, but the closer it is in time to the behaviour you want to influence, the more effective it is likely to be. It should be brief and frequent, the more often the better. For someone you work closely with, such as your secretary, it will be an almost constant process. With others, it may be daily or at least as often as you see them. (Do you see your staff face-to-face often enough? Development by memo does not work.)

The time not to give feedback is the morning when you are suffering from a heavy night, and are likely to bite anyone's head off. In most instances, it doesn't matter where you give feedback. Passing the tea area, you can touch a shoulder and praise the report you've just received, but suggest for the next one that they refine it to one sheet of A4. You can pop your head round the door of someone's office to say how pleased you were at the way he or she helped a colleague out with a problem.

Moving around your patch, you can make opportunities to turn any contact into feedback and development. Making a specific arrangement to see someone, or have them see you, creates more formality in the situation, unless there are other things to discuss as well, but there may be occasions when you want to spend more time without interruptions.

When giving feed-back on sensitive or personal matters, always do it in private.

How to give feedback is less simple. First be clear on your motives. Feedback is meant to benefit the recipient, not to relieve your feelings about their performance. If you feel angry with them, wait until you have cooled off. If you want to give them a rollicking, that's fine, as long as you recognise that that is what it is. It is not the sort of feedback which will develop them. That should come later when you feel less emotional.

Ensure to yourself and make it clear to the recipients that you are giving feedback on their performance or behaviour, not on them as people, particularly if you are giving negative feedback. If they are to benefit from your guidance, they need to retain respect for themselves and for you.

Feedback should be based on direct observation, not on inference or hearsay, and it should be based on a description of behaviour which you can both acknowledge, not a judgement on your part. Say, for example, 'We are getting a lot of disputed accounts this month,' rather than 'You're not handling the accounts properly'.

The communication should be two-way, sharing ideas on better ways of doing things and exchanging information. If you take over and just tell subordinates what to do, they don't learn for next time and you will find yourself doing their job as well as your own.

Development results when you encourage subordinates to think around the problem and explore alternatives rather than provide an answer. They are doing the job, and your answer may not be the best one anyway. Show them ways of generating information and ideas and let them work on it.

Giving and receiving feedback is an essential skill in such other development methods as coaching and delegating, but it is also very rewarding, not only for the staff but for the boss, who gets as much out of it as they do.

Resources

The brief but renowned bestseller, *The One Minute Manager* by K. Blanchard and S. Johnson (Fontana, 1983), is basically about giving feedback, but pays less attention to receiving it. Chapters in this book which help in the mechanics of giving and receiving feedback are 'Listen', 'Communicate Effectively', 'Encourage Assertiveness', and 'Know Yourself'.

12

Use Mentoring

'If each of us hires people who are smaller than we are, we shall become a company of dwarfs. But if each of us hires people who are bigger than we are, we shall become a company of giants.' These words of David Ogilvy are quoted in *Passion for Excellence*, describing how, when he had been instrumental in developing young talent in the company and he saw them rise fast and high, he would send them one of those Russian wooden dolls which have a smaller doll inside, and a succession of smaller dolls inside that. He would write these words on a note inside the smallest doll.

> To be a good mentor, as to be a good boss, you have to be prepared sometimes to see your protégé rise beyond you, and satisfy your ego with the constructive part you played in his/her success for the sake of your organisation.

It makes no small contribution to your reputation either. But it is not only high flyers who can benefit from mentoring; it can develop any grade of employee. Some organisations use the word 'sponsorship' when talking about mentoring done well.

I shall stick with 'mentoring' but point out some potential abuses as well as uses. Mentoring has more senior and usually older members of the organisation acting as counsellors, encouragers and advisers to those who do not report to them and may not even be in the same department. The elders act as a sounding board for their protégés, help them to understand the culture and mythology of the organisation, stimulate them to recognise and meet their potential, and give opportunities for them to network effectively through their own contacts.

A mentor challenges and supports his or her protégé in personal and professional matters, but particularly in longer term career development.

The process is used initially to speed the progress of high flyers through the company so that they contribute their full talents as early as possible, while absorbing the company values and culture as quickly as possible. If the right choice of mentor and protégé is made, deep and lasting relationships often result and continue through life, even after the protégé has moved up to higher things and outgrown his or her mentor. But the method has other uses, e.g. as a way of induction for new managerial staff at any level, as a way of developing any manager out of a career rut, or as a way of staff development which can potentiate the benefit of other forms of training.

But isn't this what bosses should be doing for their own subordinates? In many ways a good boss is also a mentor with a small 'm', but the mentoring relationship centres on personal and career development; on wider networking through the company, with a longer view of the protégé's progression upwards and outwards; and on personal effectiveness in the company as a whole, now and in the future.

Certainly the immediate superior should take an active interest in all of this – subordinates are not just job-holders, they are people with pasts, futures and personalities – but mentoring is not meant to undermine the subordinate/supervisor relationship in terms of current and potential performance. It is an adjunct to it with a slightly different perspective and based on a different kind of personal relationship, which, for a variety of reasons, may not be possible between subordinate and immediate superior.

Certainly, operating these two relationships does have potential for problems, e.g. in split loyalties and jealousies, but if these can be overcome, there are a number of advantages.

- By developing relationships outside the section or department, it encourages a corporate outlook and understanding.

- It enables employees' potential to be reached more quickly for the benefit of the company as a whole, and can lead to better career moves, sideways and upwards, than might otherwise have taken place.

- It can provide a source of motivation and movement for 'stuck' middle managers both as protégés and mentors.

- It provides a source of stimulation and care for an employee who may not be getting this from his/her immediate superior, whatever his/her level of ability.

- It provides the protégé with a 'second opinion', an additional source of guidance and information, particularly in matters of personal development and on aspects of the company's operations. It also enables protégés to learn from other people's experience as well as their own.

To overcome the inherent problems of this system, it has to be understood thoroughly throughout the company, and operated within the context of company values and needs. If these are not clearly understood, strongly adhered to and constantly reinforced within the organisation so that protégé, subordinate, superior, and mentor are all working for the same corporate goals, then the system can be disruptive and divisive. One of the main weaknesses apparent in some big corporations has been the development of personality cults by strong and effective mentors. Competition within the company between 'Thompson's people' and 'O'Brien's people' takes over from pursuit of a shared vision.

The basic principles of mentoring can and do take place informally in many UK organisations, sometimes based on wider family or old school tie connections. But without the formal recognition and understanding of shared purpose, particularly by the protégé's supervisor, it can be difficult to handle and is likely to have all the benefits for the protégé as an individual and few for the organisation.

Obviously the mentoring relationship must be based on mutual respect, if not admiration, and the selection of mentors is critical. They need not be the highest performers. Although emulation of example is important, inter-personal and tutoring skills are more so. To appoint a sound but 'stuck' middle manager as mentor can have spin-off in revitalising the mentor's motivation, provided he or she has not been stuck so long as to become resentful. The mentor must be sufficiently self-confident not to feel threatened by the abilities of the protégé, and yet not so strong as to create dependence. Experience in both roles has a great deal of development potential.

Mentoring as an explicit part of organisational culture and staff development policy does take up a lot of time, but it can reap returns in creating an ethos in which mutual support, learning and interpersonal skills are developed and applied to achieving a common goal. If you have experience as either a protégé, a mentor or both, it is likely to have enhanced your abilities to develop those who report directly to you. Experience in either role can also develop your staff.

Even without a mentoring system in your organisation, the cultivation of 'counsellors' outside the immediate chain of command can be of great benefit to yourself and your subordinates. It is worth encouraging such a relationship. Some managers fear that their authority may be threatened by an outside influence, but the boss who develops his or her staff has the confidence to encourage them to use all available resources to the ultimate benefit of the whole team. Therein lies their leadership strength.

Resources

The best book on the topic is *The Art of Mentoring* by Mike Pegg, Management Books 2000. It offers tools that readers can use to pass on knowledge and wisdom, to nurture talent, and to enable people to find creative solutions to challenges.

13

Prepare for Promotion

In a survey of nearly 1000 chief executives of major British companies, the researcher Charles Margerison revealed that early significant responsibility was considered the second most important factor which led to the chief executive's success. The top five factors the CEOs perceived as influencing their development as managers were:

1. ability to work with a wide variety of people
2. early responsibility for important tasks
3. a need to achieve results
4. leadership experience early in career
5. wide experience in many functions prior to age 35.

The significance of these results for you in developing your subordinates is that while the first and third factors might be considered innate qualities (although still susceptible to encouragement or repression), the other three are entirely within your power to grant.

Most managers are familiar with the Peter Principle, that in a hierarchy people tend to be promoted to their level of incompetence – and stay there. You probably chuckle as you think of some notable examples in your own organisation. But it is the bosses who bear the major responsibility for this phenomenon.

The process which enables this to happen is that of promoting people because they perform well in the jobs they do now, instead of assessing potential for the job they are being considered for. If that job happens to be their first managerial post, or one of far greater leadership responsibility, then the skills they exercise now may not be those required in the future.

Unless there is a system of preparing people for promotion and assessing their suitability 'in action', making more senior appointments is a very expensive shot in the dark. All too often, it seems to be worked on the 'Buggins's turn' principle – poor old Buggins hasn't been given a lift, so it must be his turn next. This, in spite of the fact (as everyone knows) that Buggins is only moderately competent at his present job.

To prepare for promotion, your staff need to be trained in any particular skills associated with the post, and given the opportunity to use them, to have their confidence developed by greater responsibility and regular feedback, and to be put into situations where they can exercise leadership skills. This applies equally to junior and senior posts. All of these can be developed by delegation but it must be well planned and executed with this specific purpose in mind.

Whole tasks should be delegated in such a way that subordinates can be held accountable for the outcome. Even this is never quite the same as having their own command, because there may be principles which they would wish to change if they could, but it gives them the feel of a major responsibility and enables you to assess how they handle it.

In most instances, this sort of delegation will involve some degree of risk. The size of risk that you can accept will depend on your line of business. It is a question of judgement, but the subordinate should be fully aware of and share the implications of the risk – that is part of the experience of responsibility. The freedom to make mistakes is the freedom to learn, and in many cases the amount of learning is in direct proportion to the size of the error.

Remember the story of the promising young manager who screwed up a deal which cost his company a sum amounting to six figures. When he was summoned to the chief executive's office, he wanted to get the inevitable ordeal over as quickly as possible and said to him, 'Well, I suppose you are going to fire me now, sir'. To which the CEO replied, 'Fire you? After what I've just spent on your education!'

You can drop subordinates in the 'deep end' by letting them substitute for you on occasions. Start with defined situations like meetings, and then leave them in charge while you go on holiday, delegating as much authority as you can. This has the advantage that you get feedback on the subordinates' performance from a wide range of sources up and down the line. It also demonstrates that you are not indispensable. Indispensable people don't get promoted. It is not only high flyers who can be developed in this way, but staff at all levels, and the earlier in their careers the better for them, for you and for the company.

Succession planning is more difficult in many public sector organisations, particularly in local authorities, because in most cases all posts are subject to open competition, and appointments at middle and senior levels are made by local politicians with usually little knowledge of the job itself or of selection techniques. Even in this situation, there is still value in preparing people for greater responsibilities. Their motivation and abilities are strengthened, and when appointments are being made for promotion, there will be a greater selection of better prepared and experienced internal candidates to choose from.

The chief executive of a large local authority in England set up his own scheme for temporary promotions, which had a cascade effect throughout the organisation. Middle managers from any service department can apply to work for a period of 18 months as the chief executive's staff officer, working on specific projects relating to the authority as a whole. During the same period, they attend a day release course on management skills at the local college. During their 18 months' secondment, their departmental duties are covered by their own subordinates acting up to their post – sometimes two or three for shorter periods so that the effect is spread more widely. Heads of departments have also started to use a similar method by bringing junior staff into departmental headquarters for a period of more centralised duties with greater managerial responsibility. The benefits the organisation gains from this temporary promotion scheme are:

- development of professionals in general management skills
- creation of challenging experience in leadership for junior and middle level staff
- encouragement of a corporate view and understanding as opposed to a purely departmental one
- opportunity to test out and assess people's ability to take responsibility
- a means of developing senior management of the future.

If your organisation does not have a scheme like this, you can still use the principles behind it within your own section or department. Take advantage of any staff absences due to leave, sickness, training or outside secondments to let the absentees' subordinates act up to the post with full authority. They will need to be prepared for this, with planned delegation beforehand, and receive feedback and support during the temporary promotion. But the experience can develop the potential of your whole team as well as make it easier to release people for off-the-job training or special assignments.

Discussions on preparation for promotion rarely mention the development of manual and semi-skilled personnel. There is often an impenetrable barrier between the hourly paid and the salaried jobs; between the operative posts and the supervisory posts. Such neglect not only ignores the potential for developing new skills, or skill transfer, it perpetuates the 'them-and-us' attitude and leaves people feeling trapped in dead-end jobs. It is a bad place to foster disillusionment and demotivation, for in many organisations it is the hourly paid personnel who have the most direct contact with customers, especially in the public sector.

Overcoming the barrier may require investment in training to fill basic educational gaps as well as for technical and supervisory skills. More importantly, it needs a change in attitude for a lot of bosses towards their operational work force, and much closer positive liaison with trade unions.

14

Create Exchanges and Secondments

No business these days, however large or small, operates in isolation, and the public sector can no longer afford to consider itself as set apart from the rude realities of commerce and industry. Market complexities and economic necessity create interdependence as well as competition whether we like it or not, and greater mutual understanding will make both more fruitful. There are advantages in employees of public and private sector organisations knowing more about the constraints and opportunities each has to work with; indeed a shared constraint can sometimes become a mutual opportunity. There are also benefits when companies not in direct competition are able to share their strengths with each other to the common gain. Staff exchanges and secondments are a good way of creating and maintaining cross-sector networks, while at the same time providing excellent development opportunities for subordinates.

- They gain the stimulus of working in a different environment with new people and fresh problems.
- They experience new standards, which can sharpen up perception of their own performance.
- They may gain additional skills or knowledge that can be directly applied or adapted to your section's work.
- Responding to the challenge of doing a project or filling a post in another organisation develops responsibility and leadership.
- The people you take into your department can bring a fresh outlook into your own work and act as a stimulus to the rest of your staff.
- Your subordinates can learn from their mistakes on somebody else's patch! (This is of course a two-edged sword and somebody else's subordinates will be doing the same on yours.)

Exchanges will obviously vary in length and purpose, and may be direct job-for-job and simultaneous, or be reciprocated at different times by various departments – the 'exchange' element meaning only that the parties both send and receive each other's employees at some time.

The length of exchange is important. If the period of transfer is too short, there is insufficient time for any real development to take place or significant work to be done. If it is too long, the loss of production time may outweigh the benefits. It is better to start in a modest way, with small numbers spending two to three months, say, with another organisation working on a specific project agreed in advance. Once the first placements have been completed and any problems ironed out, the return phase and subsequent exchanges can benefit from the experiences of the first.

Don't limit participation to middle and junior managers. Extend it to all employees of the enterprise: those on the shop-floor, in the offices, at counters, and on sites. Senior management and chief executives should be included too, perhaps on an exchange abroad.

A nationwide retail chain encourages all its branches to participate in exchanges with both public and private sector organisations, sometimes on a tripartite basis. One branch placed several staff in a local authority to study the divisional structure of its departments, and their local authority counter-parts worked in retail outlets to learn about customer care.

Secondments to other organisations tend to be for periods of one or two years and the person seconded takes up a specific post. They are not necessarily reciprocated, but several large companies in the UK have exchanged fairly senior personnel for long-term secondments with the civil service – an arrangement providing both sides with valuable and enduring contacts which encourage better communication, even if the individuals concerned develop beyond the foreseeable role in their organisation and take up posts elsewhere.

Secondments can be a means of developing and stimulating staff for whom there is no room on the promotion ladder. It can also be a good public relations exercise, e.g. seconding skilled staff to assist voluntary organisations.

Careful planning is essential to avoid situations where bad selection or misunderstandings result in animosity where only neutrality born of ignorance existed before. It is necessary to follow a few fundamental steps in setting up an effective exchange:

- Don't try to set them up 'out of the blue'. They need to be based on an existing relationship between organisations, or between key people within them, e.g. personnel/training staff or senior management. You may also use your own social and business contacts.

- Once you have identified one or more potential partner organisations, discover what specific skills or knowledge you can each offer as valuable to the other. There will be greater commitment if both parties can see benefits beyond that to the individuals concerned.

- If you have to convince others before going further, this is a good stage at which to seek approval. Gain initial commitment from as high up as possible – preferably the chief executive.

- Identify who in each organisation will be responsible for arranging, monitoring and trouble-shooting throughout the exchange.

- Select a wide range of projects which could be carried out in each organisation and determine the lengths and mode of exchanges.

- Work out with the personnel department all details relating to pay, allowances, entitlements, career implications, etc. for members of your staff who might be exchanged.

- Communicate the proposals as fully as possible among employees from whom you wish to select participants.

- Once the participants have been selected, bring them directly into further arrangements, e.g. refining projects in discussion with the hosts.

- Prepare and brief participants, including 2-3 days' familiarisation visits before the exchange so that they can see the environment and meet some of the people they will be working with.

- Visits abroad will require careful briefing on cultural matters if disaster is to be avoided. Seemingly simple things like certain hand gestures, for example, can have significantly different meanings in different countries!

- Maintain regular communication links with the partner organisation throughout the exchange period, and monitor progress.

- Arrange for the participants to present their projects formally in both their host organisation and back at their own work base. This could be a good occasion for some ceremony, or even a little razzmatazz to mark and reinforce the relationship between the organisations. Bring senior management and board members into the act.

- Follow up the work and development aspects with your own staff. Get them to brief you and the rest of the team on the experience, and put them in charge of arranging future exchanges for your section. This will give them further responsibility arising from their experience while helping them to maintain their new contacts.

Exchanges and secondments do need a lot of careful planning and monitoring if they are to succeed, but it gets easier after the first couple of successes strengthen the network. It can be a powerful development tool for individuals if they are well prepared, and the careful selection of projects can produce results which far outweigh the loss of output during the absence of participants.

15

Enrich Jobs

There is nothing wrong with fish and chips. It is a well balanced meal. But if the daily menu is made up of nothing else week after week, month after month, with no hope on the horizon of a meat pie, a sausage or a beefburger, then not even a dash of tartare sauce can relieve the boredom and stop you being turned off meal times.

Job descriptions, which were intended to permit a systematic evaluation of work with comparable rewards, and to give employees a clearer idea of their function and objectives, are in danger of limiting our work menus to a monotonous and rigid diet. In addition, the catch-all expression, 'any other duties which may reasonably be designated', is not a solution but a gift to the litigious.

'I'm not paid to think' must be the ultimate expression of demarcation despair, and it tells you more about the boss than the employee. Demarcation disputes are invariably more complex than they appear on the surface and often have an historical base which has long since become irrelevant to the goals of the organisation. But they are usually rooted in money, and it is always what the other guys get that is the centre of acrimony.

Money may be the reason why most of us go to work, but it is not necessarily the incentive to work harder, smarter or with more enthusiasm. It has been proved time and time again that beyond a certain essential level of security for each person, pay rates are not a major factor in motivation and development of performance, provided other rewards are available. This last proviso is the key. If the only reward people think they can get is cash in hand, i.e. they have no expectation of variety, challenge, recognition or advancement, then they will make pay the main issue and fight hard for more of it. The money helps to make up for what they see as monotonous and dead-end jobs, and because it is only a compensation and cannot in itself satisfy, they will soon be back for more. But they will be no better motivated or developed.

What tends to motivate and develop subordinates in a lasting and self-sustaining manner is whatever enriches their working lives. It is as difficult as comparing the standard of living and the quality of life. They are not the same. Given a reasonable standard of living, the quality of life as defined by each person may bear no relation to material gain – quite the reverse. Many people have given up careers with high standards of living to seek what they view as a higher quality of life elsewhere on less pay.

Job enrichment means giving scope for a higher quality of working life. It means enabling people to achieve self-development, recognition and personal growth through work which is made interesting, offers opportunities for advancement and provides feedback on their performance.

If your organisation doesn't have formal job descriptions, don't be in a hurry to call the personnel department and have them made up. They'll probably arrange to send an 0 and M specialist with a stopwatch who rushes past you in too much of a hurry to ask you what it is you are actually trying to achieve. Job descriptions should be a tool for flexibility and adaptability in achieving your goals, not straitjackets which prevent change and constrain people's potential.

If you do have job descriptions, take a critical look at them. Ask yourself 'what if' questions about what you do and the way you do it. Do they give scope for change and development, of both work and people? Do they provide goals and challenges, or do they describe duties and routine? Ensure that your people have job descriptions which enrich rather than impoverish their experience at work.

What else you can do to enrich your subordinates' jobs depends on your present situation and power base. A full re-evaluation of jobs and a reconstitution of working methods may be neither necessary nor feasible, but there is a lot a good boss can do to increase the quality of his or her subordinates' working lives without having to take over the company to do it.

Show trust
Remove petty controls; give your staff more freedom and accountability in arranging and pacing their own work schedules; increase levels for spending/ordering without prior approval; let them sign their own mail; share more information with them about the company and about your own problems and intentions at work.

Communicate and share
Use joint problem-solving rather than telling; allow staff to share in working out your job-enrichment scheme; give appraisal and feedback; seek their opinions; inform staff about company progress; advise about advancement.

Increase responsibility and authority
Delegate larger jobs; amalgamate tasks into whole job units; give clear power to achieve an end product; let them participate at meetings for which they have prepared material; require less frequent checks or longer reporting periods; let

them see and control their own error rates; give maximum self-regulation with clear knowledge of goals; grant greater discretion in decision-making.

Improve abilities and prestige

Give new, or harder, tasks to stretch abilities; let junior staff draft correspondence; let your secretary run a few meetings; enable the development of specialisms; let the best computer operator become an instructor for others; let the computer 'expert' teach you; give training and coaching; let staff know how good they are by seeing the results for themselves; consider rotation of routine or repetitive jobs on an hourly, daily, weekly basis (but don't impose it).

Enthuse

Enrich everyone's life by showing a little excitement and enthusiasm; celebrate their achievements, yours and the company's; build into job design recognition and dignity.

The strongest incentive for implementing good management ideas is doing things for other people which benefit ourselves even more – and job enrichment is no exception. The benefits to you, the boss, probably outweigh those to your subordinates:

- better motivation and job satisfaction
- increased output and higher performance
- greater knowledge of, and commitment to, company goals
- development of existing and new skills
- opportunities to assess potential in advanced tasks
- more flexible and adaptable workforce
- better job/person match becomes possible
- encourages desire for self-development/learning
- more challenge, stimulation and variety.

It's a wonder every manager isn't dedicated to job enrichment. But even those who are don't always apply it widely enough. One of the often neglected groups is the counterstaff in retail, food and service industries. These are the people in intimate daily contact with the whole purpose of the business – the customer.

Are your counterstaff given any discretion in the stock that is held? The quality of the product? The layout of the store? The handling of complaints? The ordering procedures and the time it takes to get supplies? Do you send them off to try out your competitors and identify what they do better, and have someone listen to them when they get back? Do they get a chance to specialise in a particular range of products/services, and also to try out other departments?

The other group which invariably works well below its potential and is usually overlooked when considering job enrichment and other management development schemes, or anything else for that matter, is secretaries. These days, many secretaries are more qualified than their bosses and they are often better organisers and handlers of people. Wise bosses do not feel threatened and try to keep them down, but identify and use the secretary's strengths to complement their own. Take a long, hard look at your secretary's qualifications, abilities and experience. Is he or she really using his or her full potential for the benefit of yourself and the firm? Get someone else to mind your outer office for an hour, sit down with your secretary and work out ways in which the job can be extended and enriched – ways that include not only your delegating more of your work, but also your increasing your secretary's freedom of action and responsibility.

Likewise, look at other jobs in your organisation that are slightly outside the usual hierarchical ladders – often these people are missed.

16

Stretch Abilities

Most of us spend over half our waking hours at work and getting to and from work, and yet many jobs demand only a small proportion of our talents. We have skills and aptitudes which bring us great satisfaction and fulfilment, but we are not able to use them at work. Yet a sense of fulfilment is one of the greatest forces for motivation and development.

Think of the pigeon fancier. He knows the names and personalities of each of his birds. He knows what each can do and understands all their little foibles. Before a race, he'll spend hours whispering encouragement and tenderly stroking their feathers before releasing them from the basket. When they return, he greets them with jubilation and expressions of praise and endearment. If his job allowed him to apply this commitment to managing people, what a team he would have! If only the energy and dedication that many people show towards their hobbies and leisure pursuits were to be matched by their energy and dedication towards their work activities, production would shoot up!

But there are people at work who seem to sparkle. Their apparently boundless energy and creativity become a legend – every organisation has one. They are not workaholics. It is just that their jobs enable them to apply all their talents in one way or another, and they get fulfilment from this as well as a sense of achievement for the results they produce. Sadly, they are a rare breed, but by being aware of your staff's talents and managing their application to what your team is trying to achieve, you can increase the number of your own staff who sparkle. The less you use of people's full potential, the smaller proportion of their commitment you get in return.

For people to develop, they must have challenges and demands in their jobs. It is significant in our use of language that the responsibilities of a post are frequently called 'duties', particularly in the public sector. Job descriptions should list the 'challenges' of the post. Work can be designed to stretch people's abilities and give them something to continue striving for by coaching them in higher level work or new tasks, and by delegation. This means delegating interesting assignments – even the ones you like doing best yourself.

The subordinate must share in the objective of the task and should be a party to setting both these and the targets to achieve them. It is essential that people can see for themselves an indication of their continuing progress. They also need to understand the standards expected and know when they have been reached.

People who cannot readily see a measure of progress often hoard work so that they can look over it and gain a sense of achievement that way. They keep their in-trays full because they can see at a glance how busy they are. Have you looked around your own office lately? Is your desk piled high with papers that remind you how important and indispensable you are? If so, delegate at least 60 per cent of it to your team and demonstrate how really important they are. If the tasks are new to them, stretch their abilities by coaching them in the skills required.

People meet our expectations of them. If you expect them to give you as little as they can get away with, that is what you will get. If you expect them to rise to new heights of achievement and look for more challenges in their work, they will do so – if you give the encouragement, coaching and feedback which enables them to succeed.

As with all staff development, it can only work if you know your subordinates well. There are limits to everyone's ability. They are likely to be much higher than you think, but it is important to recognise when someone has reached the full extent of what he or she can handle. If you try to stretch them beyond this, you will develop losers. Repeated failure will destroy their self-confidence, even in tasks they can do well.

Looking for talent and ways to stretch it need not be confined to a subordinate's existing or usual workload. To use all the talents of your team you need first of all to find out what they are, and then be creative in the ways you seek to develop and use them.

Make a point of talking to your people to find out what they excel in outside work. What are their hobbies, interests and specialities? See the expression on their faces when they talk about them, and work out ways of transferring these talents to their work along with their passion for it. They will welcome a chance to show off what they can do, and to enrich their jobs with things they really like doing when given a free choice.

If someone, say a young salesman, has hidden aspirations to be a writer, and scribbles in his spare time, get him to write for your company magazine or for a professional journal. It could be good publicity for your organisation too. Let him start up a regular news bulletin for your own department and distribute the good news around the company.

A keen photographer could be sent out to take pictures of your department's or company's work, compile a small exhibition or presentation sequence for recruitment talks in colleges and schools, presentations to local groups, visiting board members or customers. One of your own people will have a better eye for what should be photographed than a professional photographer who knows nothing of your business, and it gets your subordinate out to parts of the company he or she may not have seen before.

When you discover the secret cordon bleu cook among your staff, ask him or her to do the catering for the works party. If that is only once a year, why not start a departmental lunch each week or each month, or have a regular wine and nibbles review meeting for your team last thing on a Friday afternoon, and get your pet chef to prepare something special.

PCs are so available for every home nowadays that you probably have several real computer buffs in the office. Use their enthusiasm to give 'introduction to computers' training sessions to the rest of the section, or sessions involving he latest operating system or graphics package. If necessary, coach them or get them trained in instructional skills first.

There is always at least one person in any place of work who is on every local committee, and can quote the genealogies (both regular and irregular) of every family within a 20-mile radius. Put this person in charge of sending newspapers and other sources of local information to new recruits moving into the area.

The sporty types could set up interdepartmental scratch matches in anything from darts to ice hockey, and the artistic ones can have special responsibility for visual aids. They can all help with exhibitions too – make them team projects.

Good communication and presentation skills are great assets to your organisation and should be put to full use. If one of your subordinates, say, regularly gives talks out of work with an organisation such as Speakers Club or Toastmasters, for instance, and enjoys the experience, get him to coach others in the team, or let him contribute to in-company courses in the training department on a regular basis. This will also foster a good relationship with the company trainer. Make use of good speaking skills to give the right image of your company in recruitment presentations or public promotions.

All forms of staff development can increase motivation. Just being noticed has some impact, but being encouraged to use their spare time speciality at work, and thus use more of themselves, will add a new dimension to both creativity and motivation for your team.

Take up Management by Walking About and go talent spotting, join the coffee break chats, ask people if they did anything special over the weekend, and listen to their comments about what is important to them. Have a brainstorming session with your team on how many ways they can use their personal talents to enrich their jobs, their working environment and the organisation as a whole – and include yourself in the exercise.

17

Take Calculated Risks

If you manage by always being in the office, by having a permanently open door, by supervising your staff closely at every stage of their work, and by doing anything important, complex, or required for the chief executive personally, then you are already taking risks, probably uncalculated.

All these things may be appropriate on occasions, but if the result is that work manages you instead of the other way around, you risk losing direction by having insufficient time to plan and set priorities, by not being aware of what is really going on because you are not 'out on the patch' often enough, and by demotivating staff because they lack a sense of achievement through responsibility. You also risk everything you have so painstakingly built up collapsing when you are on leave or off sick with 'burn-out'.

It is not the manager's job to hold a finger in the dyke to stop the flood – he or she should be planning new and better dykes, and training others to build and maintain them.

The reason why so many managers over-supervise and smother initiative out of their staff is usually fear that their mistakes will reflect badly upon themselves. In fact, their boss and their boss's boss have not got where they are without trusting people and taking calculated risks. It is a paradox of management that the higher up the hierarchy and the more power individuals have, the more they are dependent on the competence, loyalty and integrity of others. A boss's power is only as great as his subordinate's motivation. If he or she has trained and developed good people, the risk in this inevitable dependency is far less; but it can't be reduced by close supervision or nobody would be steering the ship.

The other reason, which seems to be prevalent in the public services, is the fear of working at the boundaries of one's authority and power. Such managers use public accountability, regulations, and standing orders as stays to keep them safely well within the boundaries for fear of being seen to step out of line. They keep their head well down in the trench, which limits their own vision and cramps the style of their subordinates.

Most of us have a greater potential for responsibility, authority and power than we actually use, but it seems safer not to work at the margins and stretch the boundaries and ourselves. Many restrictions on initiative and creativity are thus self-imposed, and for the subordinates of such a manager it is even more confining.

Of course it is necessary to have adequate control. But staff are better developed and motivated when controls are exercised through objective setting, establishing measurable standards, and being delegated the authority to work within this framework, reporting only on exceptions to agreed results. Reporting by exception, coupled with proper delegation and feedback, gives employees the power to achieve and the freedom to learn.

A national fast food chain has a system for developing promising waitresses to supervisory positions, by a period of off-the-job training followed by the planned delegation of supervisory duties under the restaurant manager. One potential supervisor had on occasions found it difficult to exercise her authority over drunks and difficult customers – an essential ability in the catering trade. One evening when a well tanked-up elderly gent sat down and fell asleep while waiting for his carry-out, she found something very absorbing to do in the back kitchen. The manager, who was there at the time, briefed her about what should be done and, reminding her that it was her responsibility, went on a walk-about to other units in the vicinity.

He returned twice, but she had not been able to face up to the situation and one of the waitresses had eventually dealt with the matter quite peacefully. The manager took a calculated risk which gave the opportunity for the trainee-supervisor to learn. In fact, she learned that she could not at that stage in her career cope with the responsibility. The manager actually reduced the longer term risk of making an appointment which would not have worked, by letting the problem reveal itself. But what he did lose was a good waitress, because she left, not wanting to return to a job with lower status.

Not all control standards or risks can be reduced to easily measurable targets and quantified output, and in the management of professionals there will be areas of 'professional freedom' where standards and methods may be debatable. Controlling and calculating risks is subjective as well as objective, and your skills in it will only improve with exercise and review.

Some jobs leave little room for risk-taking by their very nature. Learning solely by experience in administering medicines, for example, would pretty soon become self-limiting through lack of customers. It is a matter of judgement and 'gut feel' how you balance risk against the development potential for the individual, and it depends on your knowledge of the person as well as the job.

Knowledge of the risk and implications should be shared by the persons undertaking the job; only in that way do they too learn how to calculate risks as well as bear the responsibility for them. It is a vital area of managerial judgement which cannot be taught or learned in any other way. Encourage them to take calculated risks by defining as generous an outer limit or bottom line as you can, and let them share the responsibility – and the glory. If they are clear on the values, and you have shared with them your vision of what really counts, this will provide them with a framework in which to have the confidence to use initiative.

Develop a positive attitude towards mistakes by using them as learning opportunities for giving feedback and coaching. Admit to your own mistakes, and use them as learning situations for your staff too. It demonstrates that you can learn from experience, and if you're big enough to admit that you're not infallible, they are less likely to hide their mistakes from you, or to keep their heads (and their ideas) well down in the trench. People will only learn from their mistakes if they feel free to admit them and discuss them.

Not only will your staff develop, but it leaves you with time to pick up those opportunities that you don't see when your head is down at the desk, or that you can't do anything about because you dare not take your finger out of the dyke.

18

Use Project Teams

A very fertile method of work for staff development, particularly in management skills, and one which is often overlooked for this purpose, is project teams. They vary in the way they are set up, but the essential feature is that they comprise a group of people from different disciplines, all working consistently towards the completion of a major piece of work, co-ordinated by a project manager.

This grouping creates a matrix structure in that the group is formed horizontally, cutting across functional divides and vertical lines of command in the hierarchy. A project team may exist for several weeks or months, depending on the task. In a very large scale project like the development of a new aircraft, the team may be in existence for several years, and its membership is likely to change. Ideally, however, the membership should be stable throughout the life of the project.

Departments of architecture frequently use a matrix structure of project teams superimposed on to a departmental hierarchy for different design projects. Such an arrangement within a department is shown in Figure 18.1.

Each member of staff is also working on other projects, with different combinations of disciplines. Each professional therefore reports to a separate project manager for each project, as well as his or her own line manager within the department.

Industry commonly uses project teams based on a product, and the composition of these teams cuts across functional departments, as shown in Figure 18.2. If it is a large or complex project, team members are unlikely to have other project or departmental responsibilities at the same time.

SECTION HEADS - ARCHITECTURAL DEPARTMENT

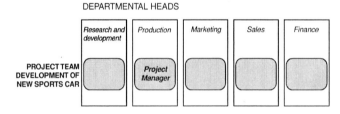

	Quantity surveyor	Landscape design	Architect section 1	Architect section 2	Structural engineer	Electrical engineer
TEAM ONE SCHOOL BUILDING			Project Manager			
TEAM TWO VILLAGE IMPROVEMENT			Project Manager			
TEAM THREE RENOVATION: NEW HEATING SYSTEM				Project Manager		

Figure 18.1

DEPARTMENTAL HEADS

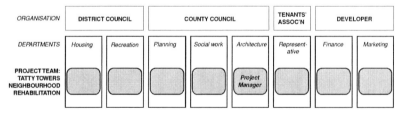

	Research and development	Production	Marketing	Sales	Finance
PROJECT TEAM DEVELOPMENT OF NEW SPORTS CAR		Project Manager			

Figure 18.2

ORGANISATION	DISTRICT COUNCIL	COUNTY COUNCIL			TENANTS' ASSOC'N	DEVELOPER	
DEPARTMENTS	Housing	Recreation	Planning	Social work	Architecture	Represent-ative	Finance	Marketing
PROJECT TEAM: TATTY TOWERS NEIGHBOURHOOD REHABILITATION					Project Manager			

Figure 18.3

A third type of project team is one that cuts across not only vertical structures and functional divides but also across different organisational divides. For example, for a major community project the team may be made up as shown in Figure 18.3.

There are obvious potential difficulties with a matrix structure in that serving more than one boss can result in divided loyalties; project managers and functional bosses may not share the same objectives, and disagree over resource allocation; and staff may find themselves overloaded with tasks from different quarters, and after some time spent on a project, may find they have lost touch with mainstream departmental work and their place in the promotion stakes.

But project teams have the enormous advantage of concentrating resources and skill. They are best used for tasks that are very complex or new; tasks that have a tight deadline or require controlled input from a range of disciplines; tasks that are large in scale or of vital importance to the organisation; or tasks in which the problem naturally extends beyond functional divides and cannot effectively be handled within the constraints of existing structures.

To operate effectively, project teams must be given the authority, resources and accountability to work through the project with the minimum of outside interference to agreed standards. As with any delegation, the objectives, and the power available to achieving them, must be clear at the outset. The role of the project manager in relation to the team, and the structural hierarchies from which it is derived, is vital.

Project teams are a rich source of experience and development. But, like any experience, it is not enough in itself for learning to take place. The learning has to be planned and deliberate, and it can be so without in any way detracting from the primacy of the project task.

If one of your subordinates is playing a part in a cross-departmental project, use it as a development tool by identifying beforehand the development potential. Regularly review progress by reflecting on the experience, giving feedback on performance, and reinforcing learning.

The general development aspects of project teams are the following.

- They engage employees in a total project from planning to completion.
- They give a wide, corporate view of the task and the operations of the organisation as a whole, by sharing work with staff from other functions.
- They enrich jobs by giving a variety of work and experience.
- They encourage independence in problem-solving by group self-direction.
- They encourage communication and team-working skills.
- They enable the specific strengths of team members to be used to best advantage.

When planning and reviewing the experience as a development opportunity for subordinates, pay particular attention to the following skills when giving feedback:

- target setting and monitoring
- problem-solving
- risk-taking
- planning
- interpersonal and influencing skills.

Project teams are also a good tool for career planning. In particular, the role of the project manager can be a challenging and enriching experience for a 'stuck' middle manager, for whom there is no available slot for upward promotion, but who nevertheless has strengths to contribute and needs to be given opportunities for further development. The role is also a useful medium for preparing professionals for management responsibilities and for assessing suitability for promotion.

If you are in the position of project manager, especially if it is a long project, use the same approach to develop your team. Coach them as individuals and as a group to build upon strengths and reduce the impact of weaknesses. For example, when holding progress meetings, if something has gone wrong, encourage the team to examine the reasons for it, especially if it is rooted in relationships and communications within the team. Only then decide what remedial action should be taken. The same learning can be derived from successes of course. The important thing is to make time for team reflection so that the learning can be identified, recognised and used in the future.

If your organisation is not geared to fully fledged inter-departmental project teams, or the work of your department does not lend itself to this as a permanent method of operating, it is still possible to gain many of the benefits of project teams by setting up short-term task forces. These need only be of a few weeks' duration, for the purpose of tackling a new or specific task within the department where the skills of several different people can be pooled to greater effect.

Alternatively, you can form a small task force which has a permanent function in addition to the normal responsibilities of its members, e.g. to monitor progress on a number of other projects, to set up and run a resource library for the department, or to be a think-tank for new products, methods or systems. But, as with project teams, the learning which happens haphazardly and unconsciously is limited; the development opportunities must be planned, looked for and reviewed.

Temporary task forces are particularly useful for giving individuals experience in leadership in a gradual, controlled way. The experience of taking charge of teams of varying size, duration and task complexity, can be geared to stretch the leader while controlling the risk of failure for him or for the task.

Some organisations use short-term projects specifically as a method of management development. The training is the prime objective rather than the task itself. But if this arrangement is to have credibility among the team members and their bosses, it must be carefully planned beforehand. There are a number of factors essential to success:

- The development purpose of the team must be clearly explained at the outset and the objectives identified.

- The project should be perceived as being relevant and of real importance to the organisation, and preferably one with corporate benefit. A real problem is an ideal vehicle, provided the risk is not so great as to attract too much interference from top management.

- Team members should be drawn from several departments or functions, and should be more or less homogeneous in status.

- The authority and remit of the team must be clearly defined.

- The size of the task and the work to be done must be realistic in terms of team members' departmental workloads, unless these can be adjusted for the duration of the project.

- The team should make a formal written and verbal presentation of results to top management, even the board of directors if it is a topic on which it would normally make a decision. The team's results must be taken seriously; if they cannot be implemented, the reasons should be explained. If there is a long delay in presenting the team's conclusions, or they are not listened to, the whole idea will lose credibility and the members of the team will feel disillusioned. Their frustration may reflect back on their mainstream work and on attitudes towards future training activities.

Some useful examples of projects are the following: implications of new technology, such as the introduction of email or an intranet; communication systems within the organisation; review of company training policy; or investigating the aftermath of the data-protection legislation.

Participation by the company training officer or other tutor is necessary to give feedback on the way the team operates as a group, to bring out learning points, to enable the team members to learn how to learn from their experiences as they develop, and to ensure the project reaches maturity (managing external forces to achieve this if necessary). A little spice can be added to this method by having two or three teams running concurrently on different projects. They can give mutual feedback on each other's performances, particularly the final presentations, and an award can be made for the best performance. If project teams are being introduced for the first time as a regular method of company working, setting up training teams like those described above is an excellent way of preparing staff for the change to a matrix structure.

You can use the same principles as a staff development tool within your own section or department, and the same considerations apply. The task must be useful and relevant, and you must show interest in the team's work and take its results seriously. If possible and appropriate, take them higher up the organisation and let the team do the presenting.

If the project is to be implemented, even better motivation and development will result if the same team can see it through to completion, or at least hold a watching brief for its implementation. If this is possible, tell the team at the beginning of the project; it will increase the impact of the whole exercise as a real contribution to the company, rather than 'just' a training exercise which need not be taken too seriously.

Training and development are not activities to leave until the order book looks full and problems have been safely resolved. The most effective way to learn is through real work – crises if necessary – and project teams, whether task-based or training-based, can be a very productive form of staff development with just a little extra knowledge and forethought by the boss.

Resources

A useful text is *On the Seventh Day* by Ian Gouge, Management Books 2000, which is essentially about the creation and management of IT projects, but which has great relevance to any project team.

19

Encourage Learning for Action

I was standing by the bar at a major conference, sipping a well-earned drink. The sessions had been stimulating but the delegates who surrounded me were far more animated and interested in their own discussions than they had been in the auditorium. 'We had a real headache trying to put that new process into operation,' 'How did you get senior management to …?' 'So, what was the real cause of the problem?' 'Yes, I had a similar situation a couple of months ago …' 'Do you really think that will work?'

People learn best from each other, by the exchange and analysis of real experiences, provided they know how to listen, and are receptive to the meaning of their own and others' experience. It is not copying what other people do which causes learning or results in better solutions, but the questions they raise, which makes people see the situation from new angles and re-examine their assumptions. Only by a continuous process of questioning can change and development take place.

The Irishman who replied to the request for directions to Ballylickey with the response, 'Well, I wouldn't start from here,' had more perspicacity than he is given credit for. By not giving the expected linear answer, he was throwing doubt on his questioner's whole approach to the logistics of where they wanted to go and how best to get there – even if his timing was not of the best. And he's right about it not being so far coming back!

It may be someone from a totally different line of business who will ask what appears at first to be an 'idiot question' which, when taken seriously, opens up a whole new approach we have been unable to see because we are too close to it (especially if we are the problem), or have been thinking in tram-lines. This does not only apply to problems, but to identifying and exploiting opportunities too.

Most of what is taught in schools, universities and business institutions is received knowledge through programmed learning. We need knowledge, data, information and even others' opinions, but the content is necessarily based on the past; the problems and opportunities in management and in society today are in constant change and may have no known answers. They may not in fact have a solution at all but must be ameliorated or managed within an acceptable balance of advantage and disadvantage to those concerned. Simply applying what was done last time to a similar looking situation may lead to disaster – few problems or opportunities are really the same, especially the more intractable and far-reaching ones.

Received knowledge is useful for solving puzzles because they always have an answer, and once you've worked it out, or learned how to cheat, you can always get the right result. But life is not made up of Rubic cubes. In addition to data and information, we need the ability to ask questions of ourselves and each other which probe the problem, explore all avenues and lead to new insights on which more effective action can be based.

This concept has been the crusade of Reg Revans, who established a method of problem-solving called Action Learning, which he describes as a management technique based on 'doing the thing'. It is standard practice in many large companies, all over the world, and most of the major management teaching institutions now incorporate the method in various forms in their syllabus. Although action learning can be applied to any problem or opportunity whether in the community or in business, it is particularly effective as a means of developing the personal and managerial attributes of those who participate.

The essential features of action learning are that the vehicle for learning is an informal group, each member of which is engaged on real work in real time (i.e. not on a course), and that the learning is geared to action – the implementation of decisions for which each participant remains responsible. It differs from project teams and quality circles in that the groups are not part of the formal organisational structure, there is no project manager or circle supervisor, and each member is equal and may be operating in totally different areas of work. Therein lie its unique strengths.

The way it works is that a small group of, say, five to six people agree to meet regularly to analyse and discuss issues raised by each of them in a frank and supportive atmosphere. Confidentiality is essential, not only from a business point of view but because without this trust comments are likely to be less than frank, and participants will not learn as much about themselves as they otherwise would. Self-knowledge is often the most significant learning which takes place.

The group, called a 'set', can be part of the same department, but greater insights are usually achieved if the members are drawn from different departments, or organisations, and are roughly on a par in terms of ability and their power to act on the decisions they take.

Each member in turn raises a problem or opportunity of critical importance to his or her work, and responds to the questions and comments of other set members. As relationships develop and trust grows within the group, the questions become more challenging and can lead, for example, to a complete rethink of someone's management style. The challenge is mutual, and so is the support in which each set member shares an equal need to seek better solutions and greater insights – what Reg Revans calls 'comrades in adversity'.

There may be a need initially to have a set adviser, someone who is not part of the group but who participates for the first few meetings with a specific remit to help the set through the growing pains of members listening to each other without defensiveness, learning to ask questions which help the other person rather than demonstrate the questioner's knowledge, being frank with sensitivity, resisting the temptation to provide instant solutions from previous experience, and not 'taking over' the problem from its rightful owner.

The set adviser need not be a specialist. It could be someone who has been a member of a set before, but whoever it is needs to be sensitive to interpersonal interactions, understand the processes that go on within groups, and able to explain and reflect back to the group what is taking place. Once the set members understand these processes well enough to be able to manage themselves with mutual benefit and know how to recognise and potentiate each other's learning, the set adviser withdraws.

There is an action learning set of five members, all at managing director level, from manufacturing, insurance, public utility, local authority and banking, which was established initially by a management college. The set adviser withdrew after six months and the set has continued totally under its own steam for several years. It meets for a whole day every two or three months, beginning with a meal the evening before to enjoy the social side of getting together, and gets down to real work first thing in the morning.

Despite what seemed an unlikely mix of disciplines initially, the set discovered a great deal in common. Over the years, some 90 per cent of the issues the members have shared have, after a more thorough analysis, turned out to be people problems, which, for reasons of avoiding the unpalatable or treating symptoms rather than causes, had gone undiagnosed until aired in the set.

The members gain a great deal of satisfaction not only from gaining new slants on their problem but on helping other set members with theirs. They have tackled numerous issues over the years, but the following examples give an idea of the range:

- A very tough negotiation with an outside organisation was of vital importance to a set member, and yet he seemed to be making no headway. During a series of discussions on the issue with the set, the other members reflected back to him the impression his personal style made upon them. He began to realise that being a 'teller' was not always effective, and has since been more flexible in the way he handles people and situations. After this enlightening experience, which he described as 'looking through a mirror without self-deception', he has applied his learning to dealing with staff and personal relationships as well.

- Critically low sales figures on a new product were a major problem for another member. Hard questioning and teasing out all the factors led to the conclusion that it was not a sales problem as he had first seen it. It was re-diagnosed as a marketing problem – the product was fine, but not what the market wanted at that time. This exercise also proved a revelation to another member: it identified an opportunity he hadn't known existed!

- One participant developed greater awareness of his capacity to take calculated risks and confidence in his own gut feel. The set's response to the way he handled problems revealed that past management training in an analysis and systems approach, and the culture of the firm he had been in for a long time, had dampened his personal flair and made him slow and cautious in decision-making. Later, when a potential career move came up, that too was put under scrutiny by his set members. Despite the consensus that it was not a good move, he listened to his instinct – the move was the best thing he ever did!

After the hard and sometimes uncomfortable questioning from the group, each member makes his or her own decisions and takes action for which he or she is totally responsible; but the actions themselves are also reported back for further critical discussion, which leads to more learning. Just as much learning results from carrying through the action and reflecting upon it as a set, as from the diagnosis of the problem, for both the owner of the problem and the rest of the set.

Honest and unselfish feedback is perhaps one of the greatest means of development which action learning offers. A group of headmasters who had been attending a series of week-long courses on management believed they had reached a fruitful relationship in which they could talk frankly with each other. They decided to form an action set, independently of the programme they were following, and had a set adviser sitting in with them informally for their first half dozen meetings. Their comment to the set adviser was that they now knew what real frankness and mutual support was – it had been an eye-opener on what they could discuss and learn together. Even in the early stages, there were spin-offs in the way they handled their work and their colleagues back at school.

Have you ever wished there was someone you could trust to give you unbiased and honest feedback on your management style – without any risk to your promotion? Or wanted to bounce an idea off a colleague you knew would be frank and keep your confidence? Or longed for a totally fresh viewpoint on what you were trying to achieve? Or wanted a method of developing your staff which did not take them away from the real work of the section nor give them problems of re-entering work after a period of off-the-job training?

Action learning sets can comprise any type of staff, but are especially effective in developing the following skills in managers at all levels:

- ability to listen critically
- ability to accept and give personal feedback
- interpersonal skills
- diagnostic and analytical skills
- creative problem-solving
- self-awareness and self-management
- ability to recognise and promote learning for themselves
- ability continually to review, question and appraise – the processes from which growth and development arise.

You can adapt the method to suit different situations. For example, it can be used to create a particularly strong spirit of interdependence in a work team, to arrive at greater understanding of each other's roles when new groupings are formed as a result of restructuring, to encourage staff who each work on different aspects of a wider common goal to work more closely towards it, to bring a fresh perspective on work by having someone in a set from other organisations, to strengthen interpersonal and problem-solving skills of certain of your team, or to develop staff for promotion.

If you wish to develop action learning, proceed as follows:

- Find out if any of your business or social contacts have been members of action-learning sets and talk to them about the idea.
- Consult the company training officer. He or she may have information on action-learning networks, or be able to act as a set adviser for your own staff.
- Discuss the idea with your team and see how they feel about it. Consider sets within the department, with other parts of the organisation and with outside organisations.

Remember the following points:

- Participants must take up set membership willingly, and have a high personal commitment to the group.
- The problems or opportunities tackled must be real and significant to the individual's work, and members must have power to act on their decisions, or clearly understand the bounds of their authority.

Then take the initiative in forming an action-learning set in which you will be a member.

The whole idea is deceptively simple, but achieving the desired results is not easy, and takes a lot of hard work and commitment. Those who have participated in sets wax lyrical about the benefits they have gained and the contacts they have sustained sometimes years after the set itself has dissolved. But they will also tell you that the kind of learning that results in significant change and development can be personally disruptive, uncomfortable and even painful at times – all of which is shared by set colleagues. Training and development experiences which do not cause some personal discomfort and self-questioning may be useful at the conceptual and knowledge level, but are unlikely to result in lasting change that has real impact on performance or personal growth. Breaking through the armour of complacency always has to hurt a little.

Resources
To return to the source, try *The ABC of Action Learning*, R. W. Revans (Chartwell Bran, 1983), but it is quite a big read.

20

Consider Quality Circles

It may come as a surprise to learn that quality circles have been around since 1962. From their origins in Japan, they spread to the United States and later to the UK and were taken up by some big names. These were not just dedicated followers of fashion. The method has snowballed and pay-back has been high.

Over the last 40 years, quality circles have been created in every kind of enterprise. There are successful examples in heavy industry, manufacturing, banking and commerce, retail and hi-tech industries.

There have also been notable failures, and it is not the kind of scheme you can try to introduce a second time. But the failures have resulted from lack of commitment at some level of the organisation, inadequate introduction of an idea which can represent a major change in working methods, or incompatibility with the company culture, rather than weaknesses inherent in the idea itself.

Basically a quality circle is a group of workers, all reporting to the same supervisor or foreman, that meets under the leadership of the supervisor to identify, analyse and work out solutions to work problems. The numbers in each group usually range from five to ten. Because a basic tenet of the idea is that it is voluntary, not everyone in the supervisor's group is necessarily a member.

The voluntary aspect applies also to supervisors, who obviously need to be approached first (unless of course they have suggested the idea), because if they do not want to take it on, it cannot be done successfully. Every other level of the organisation from middle management to the chief executive must also want it or the idea is likely to fall flat on its face and leave more problems behind it than the company had in the first place. Even after the groups are in operation, there is no compulsion from one meeting to the next. This freedom generally ensures a high level of commitment to attend and participate. The successes have given pay-back ratios of benefits to cost of around 8:1 – even 15:1 in a few cases. These are a reflection of improved methods, better solutions, savings on waste and materials. But it was the associated staff development which made these more quantifiable measures of achievement possible.

Quality circles have enormous potential as a method of developing employees.

- They develop more positive attitudes towards even repetitive or routine work, not as a result of manipulation but because the method genuinely creates higher expectations of the workforce. It assumes they can not only identify but solve problems which management may not even be aware of.

- They enter more into the wider implications of their role in the total end product and operations of the company. The goals are shared by the members of the group in mutual concern for their own output, but they are able to share in the company's goals too.

- Taking on more responsibility for the quality and quantity of their contribution to the company's performance results in less buck-passing of problems. Given the freedom and power to work out their own solutions, they are more willing to accept that it might be their problem. In this climate, problems produce opportunities and solutions, not blame.

- Both skills and knowledge are developed because meetings are structured to encourage creativity and rational analysis in problem-solving, skills which can be widely applied to any aspect of work. Groups brainstorm to identify problems, and in working out solutions, have to collect, analyse and present hard data, including cost benefit, for which preparatory training is given.

- They become more aware of the cost of faults, and the comparative benefits of different materials and methods of working, and are inclined to depend less on 'that's the way it's always been done around here' to justify their opinions.

Of course, on occasion the circle's analysis will reveal a problem or shortfall in management, and this is where shared goals and commitment to the method are essential. It no longer becomes adversarial management, 'them against us'. Both sides must be willing to face the facts and take appropriate action to meet agreed goals. The results are thus seen as everybody winning, workers and management, rather than a case of management with egg on its face.

One of the most widespread training spin-offs has been in the improvement of communication skills. Verbal and written communication is developed by regular purposeful discussion, compiling notes on meetings, and drawing up data for presentation to management when solutions require higher authority. The greater ease in communicating creates a virtuous circle of better understanding, more acceptable feedback and more willingness to communicate on all sides. Obviously, this forms the basis of a wide range of both management and development benefits to the whole organisation – but only if the rest of the organisation is committed enough to listen and communicate honestly. It has the potential for making communication genuinely two-way and mutually comprehensible.

Because of the voluntary factor, the membership of groups tends to be fairly constant, and the regular interaction over shared objectives, together with the application of improved communication skills within the group itself, are strong forces for developing fruitful group dynamics. This can produce better relationships generally between group members, as well as more effective teamwork when they are engaged on other tasks. For this to happen, a great deal depends on their supervisor (who leads the group discussions). The meetings themselves should not be expected to resolve long-standing conflicts of interest or personality. Where difficulties in relationships are identified by the group as a cause of work problems, they may be able to approach it in an analytical way and even resolve it, whether by changes in attitude from greater understanding or by agreed transfers. But this is a difficult task for most groups, particularly in their early stages. In fact it is sometimes underlying difficulties in group relationships which lead to failure of individual quality circles. Where team work is essential to performance, this exposes a major problem in the workplace which cannot safely be ignored, with or without quality circles.

Development and motivation are very closely linked. The motivation resulting from the 'win:win' principles of quality circles, the power of members to influence their own work, the ability to solve problems which limit their performance, and the sharing of goals, are all forces likely to increase the amount of learning and development which group membership facilitates.

But staff development must encompass all employees. To prevent the exact opposite effects on those who have chosen not to be members of a quality circle, careful attention must be given to keeping them informed of the group's activities and avoiding any suggestion of 'separate lodges'. A vital function of the supervisor is to maintain responsibility even-handedly and openly for all those reporting to him or her. This includes identifying and stopping pressure by group members for others to join or indeed for any member to leave the group.

The same development benefits are gained by the supervisors, but, in addition, they have the opportunity to grow in confidence, and to improve skills of leadership and management. These skills are particularly important for first-line supervisors to acquire, and while they can be readily learned, given commitment and opportunity, they are extremely difficult if not impossible to teach.

Introducing quality circles also provides some specific opportunities for developing middle managers from other parts of the organisation, e.g. in the role of facilitator. The start-up period for quality circles can be three to four months. During this time, induction for all levels of management takes place, and a great deal of training for potential group members and supervisors. Once a group begins its first meetings, a 'facilitator' sits in with the group for part of its sessions during the first two or thee months to make sure the learning process continues while the group is in action. He or she will tutor and demonstrate discussion skills, for example, explain to the group how or why something has gone wrong in achieving its objective, and generally ease the process of its mutual problem-solving. Learning to keep the discussion relevant can take a little time. A quality circle can too easily become a club for picking the winner of the 2.30 at Newmarket, but the only winners you want are solutions to problems. Gradually the facilitator removes him- or herself from the group.

Ideally the facilitator should be an experienced member of the company with a flair for handling groups and getting along with people. Facilitators too are trained in the use of quality circles at the beginning of the exercise, and the experience can be an ideal medium for developing junior or middle managers for positions of greater responsibility and leadership, e.g. it could form a temporary assignment as part of a promotion plan.

Unlike many other methods of staff development, the implementation of quality circles will not rest solely with you. Your commitment and skills, however great, are insufficient on their own, or even when matched by those for whom you are responsible. The introduction of quality circles has implications throughout an organisation and can amount to a major change in orientation.

Their successful introduction and continued operation depend on the following factors:

- management's desire for genuine two-way communication and participation by the workforce; workers' desire to increase company performance through their own development and actions

- a management style within the organisation which is compatible with the kind of relationships, communication and implementation which will result from the activities of quality circles

- commitment from management at all levels to the principles of quality circles and to the implementation of their solutions wherever practicable, and commitment both from group members and non-group members to the methods and results

- adequate resourcing for start-up costs and for implementation of action recommended by groups

- thorough training of employees at all levels, and skill training for all those directly participating, either by in-company trainers or in close partnership with external training providers

- time to allow groups to develop, and for their continuing operation.

It is wise to start with a pilot scheme and run it for eight or nine months before embarking on a full-scale introduction.

A decision to consider quality circles will obviously call for research into likely cost benefits, existing performance levels, and future development plans for the organisation. But like the little girl with the curl in the middle of her forehead – when she was good, she was very, very good; when she was bad, she was horrid! Even the most enthusiastic bosses should consider the essential background requirements before deciding that quality circles are the best way to develop people and improve performance in their organisations.

Resources

A very thorough account is given in *Quality Circles: a practical guide*, Mike Robson (Gower, 1982).

21

Be Flexible

Each person we work with, deal with, and meet is unique. Despite this, or perhaps because of it, we use many categories and stereotypes as a shorthand to describe people and to make some sense of the bewildering variety of humanity. There is no harm in creating our own sense of order in this way, but the danger is that we begin to impose our mental constructs on others, and constrict people to fit into the pigeonholes we have created by seeing only that which fits, and being blind to characteristics which do not.

Stereotypes, by definition, limit our perception of people, and the differences they ignore are often the most significant and exciting features of an individual. The methods and expectations of the workplace frequently reinforce these limited views of what people are and can be, and, in doing so, they diminish people and prevent development.

Rigidity in our perception of people can lead to the following commonly held assumptions about subordinates:

- Women get too emotional to manage others, especially other women.
- 'Successful' women are aggressive and butch.
- Accountants are not good with people.
- Engineers are poor communicators.
- Redheads are short-tempered.
- People who speak with a regional accent are not quite as clever or sophisticated as those who do not.
- Men are chauvinists.
- People with a physical disability are not as intelligent as the physically fit.

There are many other stereotypes. These are some of the most offensive and widely held and they can influence, sometimes unconsciously, not only our general attitude towards subordinates but the amount of responsibility we are prepared to give them and our expectations of their performance.

Numerous pieces of research have proved that in general, whether teaching students or managing employees, we get what we expect from people. Bosses who express high expectations of their staff, and provide the training and feedback necessary, are more likely to get a high performance than those who make it clear that they don't think their people are capable of much.

The world of comedy would be lost without its stereotypes of nagging wives, abominable mothers-in-law, and thick policemen – not to mention Englishmen, Irishmen and Scotsmen. But there is no place for them within your team, or within the workplace at all. In fact, such limited perceptions of customers and clients can lead to disaster in servicing and marketing as well.

Attitude towards subordinates is not the only flexibility required to develop them to their full potential. Many managers confuse consistency with rigidity. To be unchanging in approach, whatever the situation or whoever the person, results in managers who are effective only in those situations to which their style is applicable.

Managers who can adapt their approach to changing circumstances and the different needs of individual employees can be effective in a wide range of situations, moreover, they can still be consistent where it matters, i.e. in the values reinforced, the goals set, and the standards of performance expected.

There are numerous rigidities in working life which are taken for granted, and the limitations they can place on productivity, initiative and individual development go unrecognised. Trying to control too much too far down the line is one major cause, and failing to challenge petty rules and things that have 'always been done this way' is another. Many workplace rules about time, place and methods of working are out of date in the present context of rapid social and technological change. We lead increasingly complex lives. Companies and institutions must learn to adapt to this complexity if they are to enlist employees' full commitment to their objectives.

The following suggestions may well be worth a few battles with the personnel department, your boss, or even your own set ideas – bearing in mind that what you are really responsible for is results rather than being your subordinates' keeper:

- Let people work at home occasionally if their circumstances require it, if they want peace for a particular assignment, if they are at their personal best from 11 pm onwards, or to give them variety. (Remember it's results that count, not being in the building from 9 till 5.)

- If your organisation does not work to flexi-time, find out if it can be introduced. In the meantime, arrange as much informal flexibility in starting, finishing and lunch times as you can get away with, while still concentrating on results and maintaining whatever basic cover is really necessary. If your staff get 'caught' by a clockwatching member of the Board, defend them and launch into eulogies about the advantages of flexi-time – you may find yourself promoted for results-orientated initiative.

- Give everyone at least one week a year for personal development in an activity and place of their own choice, provided they can justify their objectives and report back to you on their achievements afterwards. It could be something in the community, in another firm, or an Outward Bound experience. (Locations such as Hawaii, Cannes and the Maldives should be examined carefully!)

- Allocate subordinates a percentage of their working time to develop ideas, carry out research, or pursue a particular interest of their own, which, while related to the objectives of the organisation, is not necessarily a regular part of their remit or workload.

- Encourage flexible attitudes in those who report to you by asking them, 'Given a free hand, what would you change around here?' – and listen. Ask them 'what if' questions about their own work, to encourage them to think about contingency planning and coping with uncertainty and change.

- Resist pressures to appoint new recruits because (a) their profile matches that of the previous incumbent, (b) they are built in your own image, (c) they comply with the company clone, or (d) the personnel officer insists they are the only choice.

- Never say 'no' to a new idea from one of your subordinates for at least 48 hours and without bouncing it off someone else.

- Critically review the rules and regulations you have always adhered to and managed by. Ask yourself, 'Does this contribute positively to results?' and 'Does this inhibit the development of my staff?' If the answer to the first is 'no' and to the second 'yes', take steps to get it changed.

- Evaluate all forms, registers and listings your staff have to use, particularly those which control their activities and movements – development arises from trust, and the dignity of self-responsibility. Manage by results rather than regulations.

- Be a one-person revolution on red tape and petty restrictions – you will soon find others joining in.

In our changing times, flexibility is the only way to be ready to adapt positively to contingencies as they arise. In an environment in which values and goals are clear, and learning is encouraged, it will also provide renewed opportunities in which you and your subordinates can develop your own unique potential to contribute as workers and people.

22

Stimulate Creativity

What if, next Monday morning, the janitor chaired the management team meeting and the chief executive supervised the company car park? The chances are that the chief executive would learn a lot about the company's employees, and the janitor would raise some unanswerable questions.

Creativity is about gaining new insights by daring to contemplate the impossible. It is not the same as intelligence. It is seeing things from an unexpected viewpoint, unfettered by the constraints of assumption. It requires the permissiveness of surrealism – allowing originality to provoke new images of reality without the straitjackets of linear thought and received knowledge on which we are all reared.

Can managers, those paragons of order, control and timeliness, tolerate the seeming chaos of turning situations on their heads for the sake of creativity? Can local government escape the tyranny of the committee cycle? Industry too has its tyrannies. But, in both, the limitations are more self-imposed than real. We wear them like chain-mail which both protects, and weighs us down to prevent too much exertion. More than tolerate, we have to find a way to incite creativity and innovation if we are to survive the challenges of our time.

Those who are creative may also have the ability to harness the energies and resources necessary to implement their new ideas, i.e. to innovate as well as to invent. But the two do not necessarily go together and any successful team must include both forces within it.

You cannot make people creative by telling them, or giving them bonus payments. Some people are inherently more creative than others. But for many of us, our natural creativity has been repressed so thoroughly by formal education that we no longer realise we have it. So how can bosses stimulate creativity and innovation in their subordinates – and in themselves? There are two things you can do – neither of them easy. You can appoint people with a track record or potential for creativity and/or innovation, or you can create an environment in which people's potential for both will flourish.

The head of a major international cosmetics company claimed that he always recruited classicists to his senior executive posts because they were trained to think critically. He hired brainpower not skills, on the basis that the former was an invaluable innate quality, while the latter could be learned – preferably within his company's own culture. He had a point. But by turning his insight into a rule, he was imposing artificial limitations upon the creative recruitment of creativity! It is so easy to be tied down by assumptions which confine the possible. There seems to be a natural desire within all of us to operate well within the security of these boundaries and miss so much of what is outside.

If you can recruit people with a proven record of creativity or innovation, there is a good chance, given the right environment, that these qualities will continue under your management. But despite sophisticated psychometric testing, it is impossible to judge the potential of either with any degree of accuracy. Changing recruitment policy will help if it can free you from the rigidity of enlisting from the same traditional sources and disciplines that you and every other company in your line have always used. Take a few calculated risks. Try some fresh blood from unlikely places. You can always hedge your bets with contracts which give you the option, and by not always backing the same stable.

During a three-month exchange of junior managers between a local authority and a subsidiary of an international electronics manufacturer, the managing director was surprised at the extent to which the local government managers 'blossomed' in the entrepreneurial atmosphere of his company. It revised his own attitudes towards sources for recruitment.

To establish the environment in which creativity and innovation can flourish, you may have to wield some influence outside your own chain of command, like getting rid of the work study officer who observed the drawing office of an architects' department for a day and complained about the amount of time that was spent just sitting and doing nothing. 'Thinking' was not on his activity list! The following suggestions may be helpful:

● Expect your subordinates to be creative; look out for it and encourage it. Ask them what they think and encourage them to question too. You'll be surprised just who has the ideas on the most unlikely topics.

● Be prepared to listen to what they say. That means not laughing out of court even a crazy idea without thinking about it, or better still getting others in the team to do so. The sweetest words to any boss should be 'You know, I've been thinking about ...', because a good leader is prepared also to be led, and is respected all the more for it.

● When delegating work, don't be rigid about how your subordinates achieve the objectives you have agreed. A balance must be struck between control and freedom, so seek to control only the standards, and give free reign to imaginative implementation. Whatever legal or moral constraints have to be observed in the process should be built into the agreed standards.

● When arranging team briefings or staff meetings, where possible do not mix on the same agenda routine items on past or current progress with items requiring creative contributions on future planning. The mind tends to tune into the discipline required of particular timescales, and the analytical faculties for assessing the past or reporting on results and costs are unlikely to switch easily to free thinking.

● Give your people as much time and resources as you can negotiate for experimentation and creative activity, i.e. activities which cannot necessarily be justified on the strict criterion of existing production schedules or routine workloads. A certain amount of trust is necessary here, but without it you don't get responsibility.

● Get your people to hold regular brainstorming sessions with or without your presence.

The usual method for brainstorming is to identify a problem. Restate it a few times until you are satisfied that all the angles are understood, and that you have the problem not the symptom. Select a re-statement which begins 'In how many ways can we ...', and then suspend judgement while everyone calls out any idea that comes into their heads. The essential part is to suspend judgement. No one should be allowed to question or ridicule any idea. The whole point is to get everyone to let their imagination work without inhibition while somebody writes up the ideas – which should be done at random and not as lists which make people think in sequential, straight lines. One person's idea will spark off others and the sessions are usually a great deal of fun. A good boss should not be afraid of fun: it's a great motivator as well as being good for creativity. Don't be afraid of short spells of silence even if they feel longer than they are: it's productive thinking time. When you're sure everyone has dried up, halt the session. Depending on how creative everyone is feeling, it can take 10 to 20 minutes.

Only when the freewheeling has finished, should you start to analyse the ideas and select priorities for further investigation or even further brainstorming. Keep the analysis stage in small groups for as long as possible, and limit the assessment of one person – e.g. yourself – to the very last stage if a final decision has to be made by one person. You don't have to wait until you have a problem to brainstorm. You can use the 'what if' question to practise creative thinking regularly, or just to 'see' what you are doing, where you are going and what might be two steps ahead. 'What if the market for our 'rising star' plummets next week?' 'What if we were bought out next month?' 'What if I wasn't around for the next 6 weeks?'

Brainstorming is not just a gimmick. The combination of lifting routine rigidities and group activity produces results. Continuing as far as possible in groups during subsequent phases is important too. The initial idea may not be what is useful at the end of the day. But it may spark off the creativity of another member of the group, not to refine the original idea but to come up with something totally different. You also need a mix of creative and innovatory talents working together so that good ideas can be followed through by 'champions' who are prepared to be unpopular and bend the rules in pursuing their commitment.

A simple exercise which demonstrates to management students the value of group participation in creativity is to put a plastic cup on the table and ask the group to work entirely on their own, by jotting down as many different uses for it as they can think of in one minute. Then go round the group listing them all, ignoring duplications. In any group of, say, eight, if you ask each individual how many different ideas they come up with, the average is around nine, but the combined list for the whole group is always around 45. You can use this kind of exercise as a warm-up session to get ideas flowing before your main brainstorming.

You never know where an idea will come from. Art Fry, the man who brought those little self-adhesive and removeable notes – Post Its – to every discerning manager's desk, said of those who both invent and innovate like himself: 'We are trying to do things that are different and trying to do things that people don't really understand yet and you're not sure you understand them yourself'. Fry's success depended heavily not only on the loyalty and support of his boss but on access to corporate funds, technology, manufacturing facilities and marketing channels. The original idea came from his desire to mark up page numbers securely in his hymnal during choral practice, without damaging the pages. But in getting the early development to fruition, he took advantage of corporate policy that gave all technical personnel 15 per cent of their time to work quietly on ideas of their own. Art Fry's drive and entrepreneurialism can hardly be described as 'working quietly', but no one is complaining, least of all his boss.

Give your subordinates as much outside variety and stimulation as work schedules will allow:

● Look out for seminars and exhibitions. Send two people rather than one because they will enhance each other's experience, and make sure they report back to their colleagues and yourself afterwards.

● Make opportunities for office and production staff to meet customers and clients – put them out with a salesman for a day, take them to a marketing convention or a council meeting, or send retailing and service personnel to see the planning and production side.

- Select administrative staff to spend a few weeks on exchange with their counterparts in other departments. They will see how their role relates to the rest of the company, and this will stimulate ideas about how they carry out their own work.

- Encourage small and constant creative endeavour in everyday routine work. If ideas fail, praise the endeavour and coach for better results next time.

- Be enthusiastic about your subordinates' work, even routine work. Of course it has to be genuine, but if you're paying someone to do a job, it must be worth doing and have value in the general scheme of things. If it doesn't, why should the job exist?

Creativity needs time for thinking. We can be thinking subconsciously while doing other tasks, taking a bath or even during sleep. But if your subordinates work in an atmosphere where they have to 'look busy' the whole time, or are expected to race through their work every hour of the day like whirling dervishes, they will have little opportunity or energy to be creative. Thinking should be a legitimate and encouraged activity – that goes for the boss too. Rushing headlong into a job without sufficient thought can lead to inadequate decisions which can cost a lot of time later on in putting things right.

If getting a new idea off the ground takes cutting through red tape or twisting a few arms at the top, be supportive and loyal to your subordinates, even if a new idea does not always work out. If you let them down, they won't come to you with their next inspiration – they'll take it to your competitors!

Resources

Creativity cannot be acquired from books, but the following original works will stimulate the way you think and could unleash unknown potential: *Use your Head*, T. Buzan (BBC Publications, 1982) and *Lateral Thinking*, Edward de Bono (1970). de Bono's *Serious Creativity* (HarperCollins 1993) and The Creative Manager by Roger Evans and Peter Russell (Unwin Hyman 1989) both have useful ideas.

23

Encourage Personal Development

Employees, unlike Topsy, don't 'just grow' unless some responsibility for encouraging the process and making it possible is taken by their bosses.

Personal development encompasses the whole person. It is more than technical or professional competence. Although it requires the development of skills, learning and acquiring them does not in itself guarantee personal growth. It is an area many bosses shy away from because it is not so definable and measurable as job skills, and yet if employees are not enabled to develop to their full potential as people as well as post-holders, the resources they can bring to the organisation are diminished. The kind of abilities which determine personal development are those to do with our sense of worth in relation to colleagues and the organisation as a whole, the extent to which we feel we have the power to steer our own progress, the ability to determine personal as well as work goals and confidence in our capacity to achieve them, how we relate to the environment around us, and whether we feel competent in managing ourselves.

It is obvious from the above description that the energy for achieving this has to come from the individual. Personal development has to be a self-generated activity. But like any learning, the opportunities for it can be ignored, encouraged or stifled by those with the greatest influence – the bosses.

This is an area where staff development and motivation merge into each other. Neither can be done from the outside – people can only develop themselves, and they can only motivate themselves. The lack of one usually implies the lack of the other. The action which the good boss takes is to identify the blockage to personal development, and create the conditions under which subordinates can motivate and develop themselves with the aid of counselling, coaching and feedback.

The blockages may be within the person themselves and tackling them will need a bit of horse sense from the boss. Consider the following types of employee.

The trekking pony

This is the employee who has been treading the same beat for so long he or she is virtually working in a trench. They are never going to win the Derby or even the local gymkhana but they may be around for a number of years to come, and their contribution, particularly in terms of ideas and appropriate judgement in times of change, will decrease as the years go by unless you can stimulate some growth. They are not the most able of subordinates, and, depending on how long they have been plodding the same route, will be resistant to a new order.

Create small changes and challenges in their work, give a lot of feedback and reward for even small positive deviations from the well-worn path. The increased interest and expectations will themselves help to take the blinkers off.

The hack

An able, and at one time a promising mount, he or she has been turned off from work, probably as a result of disappointment over a promotion, an unsatisfactory relationship with superiors, or by working in the wrong job. Despite untapped potential, he or she now does the work that has to be done with no great enthusiasm. Getting little sense of reward, the employee is trapped in a vicious circle.

The constraints to growth are often self-imposed. To account for their predicament, the hacks will convince themselves that they are powerless to do anything about it, 'they' up above are to blame, and this resentment can spread to those around them. Because these are basically able people, the pay-off for effort in restarting the growth process can be great. The boss has to get close enough to understand what has turned them off, to counsel them to see the snaffles they have put on themselves, and be prepared to help them break out. This may call for a planned series of development activities, even a different work role. But the important thing is to help the hack see that things can change and that he or she has the power to make it with your support.

The racehorse

The highly qualified fast-riser in the organisation may be the last person you think needs special attention to ensure personal development, but the danger is he or she may become over-specialised and develop a limited view of the organisation. Unless fast-risers' outlook and understanding are broadened, they reach top management with tunnel vision which takes no account of the needs and aspirations of the rest of the work force. Impatient and arrogant, they are unlikely to be aware that there is anything they need to learn. The boss must increase their self-awareness by creating challenges which will convince the racehorses to their own satisfaction that areas of personal growth have been neglected. Situations requiring sensitivity in interpersonal skills may be a good place to start!

These may be extreme examples though nonetheless real. The rest of your stable will also have potential for growth, if only because those who have influence on so much of their lives at home, school, college and previous employers, develop selectively what suits their purpose and whole areas are left fallow until the discerning boss recognises the need and provides the means to release and develop them.

Once you've broken through the block, there are numerous things to encourage growth – this book is full of them. The essential thing is to break through the barrier to enable subordinates to see for themselves that they have stopped growing, while at the same time offering the encouragement and the environment in which they can see what they can do about it.

But often it is not the subordinate who has stopped his or her own growth, but bosses who don't like competition, or wouldn't recognise potential if they fell over it, or the organisation, which doesn't like people to cause ripples, or is not sufficiently interested in its human resources to care whether they reach their potential or not. These blockages may be easier to recognise, but more difficult to dismantle. In many ways, organisations and bosses get the subordinates they deserve. Bright employees who realise the kind of environment they are in will leave, and those who can't will simply tune-out for a quiet life and become marginal in a variety of ways – the wastage goes unrecognised and uncosted. For many companies, it is the unseen weight they drag around with them, and when the inevitable happens, they blame the last straw, whether it is a merger, a shift in the market or an unfavourable swing in exchange rates. Being unaware, they never learn until it is too late.

Awareness is the greatest gift you can give to your subordinates. Without it there is nothing you, or they, can do about development of any kind. As with so many things, personal development is one of the most important areas and it is also one of the most difficult.

A positive outlook to self-evaluation has to be a continuous process, because our goals and aspirations alter with changes in life stage and what is going on around us. A good boss who values and understands his or her people can help this process by demonstrating positive attitudes towards them and by being willing to counsel and coach them. The following checklist will help you to encourage self-development in your subordinates:

- Identify and release blockages to growth by appraisal, feedback, and by counselling through unpalatable revelations.

- Provide challenge and stimulation in work; make your expectations known.

- Encourage self-awareness by the use of questionnaires and instruments, reflection, and new experiences which test people out and awaken their curiosity and desire to learn.

- Reward success and learning, however small, so that people feel how good it is to grow and develop.

- Encourage subordinates to think about their short-, medium- and long-term goals and alternatives, and to make personal plans.

- Encourage them to record their own personal achievements at work and outside, and to measure the attainment of their goals.

- Personal and career development includes choice as well as planning. Ensure they have information about openings and alternatives available to them; increase these choices as far as possible.

- Help them to discover how they learn best and provide information for them to do so.

- Get them to help in planning their own development; let them try various activities as 'tasters' to broaden their horizon and help them to identify the way and direction they want to develop.

- When thinking about your subordinates, think about whole people with pasts and futures, and be aware that you see only a part of their potential unless you look for it.

- Convince them and yourself that self-management begins by believing we can achieve it.

- Take a critical look at your own management style, and the culture of the organisation – do they block people in, or encourage them to grow?

Asking discerning questions is one of the best ways to encourage self-awareness. Try the following on yourself, and then on your subordinates:

- What are my main strengths and weaknesses?
- What opportunities are there for me in the future?
- What am I most afraid of?
- What have I achieved in the last 6 months that I am most proud of?
- What didn't I achieve? Why?
- What are my six most important goals over the next 12 months? (Be specific.)
- What do I need to learn to enable me to achieve them?
- How, when and where am I going to learn it?
- Keep a detailed diary for at least two weeks, then ask yourself, what did I spend most of my time doing?
- Are those the things that are most important to me?
- What do I most want to change? How am I going to do it?

Remembering that personal development has to cover the whole individual and that it is the same personal 'package' that goes to work and sits in front of the telly, or digs the garden at home, let your answers to the questions encompass your social and personal as well as your working life.

Resources

Have a look at *Build Your Own Rainbow*, by Barrie Hopson and Mike Scally –
it allows you to work through a whole range of personal development exercises
to assist in career and personal planning. Management Books 2000.

See also *Career Development*, by Tricia Jackson (CIPD).

24

Career Plan

'They then change from aiming at the maximum possible to the minimum excusable.' (Anthony Jay in *Management and Machiavelli*) The 'they' referred to are employees who have worked out that they are not going to go much further, and the small increase in pay they might get is not worth the effort on their part.

There are numerous reasons why people get 'stuck' in organisations. Sometimes it is lack of forward planning by the organisation itself of its own future development, inadequate expertise in the manpower department, or the employee's own boss. There was a case of a boss who relied so heavily upon one of his specialist middle managers that when he was asked to give references for outside appointments, he would write them in that ambiguous way that leads people to think they should be reading between the lines, and even successfully blocked an application for internal promotion.

Blocking subordinates' promotion is self-defeating. In this case the manager learned to use different referees and left anyway for a better position in a different company. These things do not stay hidden for long, and the demoralising effects on the rest of the team can be disastrous. Apart from demonstrating a 'mean streak' in the boss, it revealed over-dependency, insecurity in the ability to develop new people and a distinctly selfish attitude to the welfare of the company, whose success should also be that of the managers within it.

To develop their skills and potential, people need to feel they have somewhere to reach into, new challenges to face, and further recognition to earn. This need not necessarily be linear progression upwards in a hierarchy. Increasingly, organisational structures are becoming leaner, constricting opportunities for climbing the ladder. Career planning must encompass these changes and ensure that staff have incentive for self-development even where there is no upward mobility.

Career planning has to form part of the longer term company strategy – the human resources manager, and probably professional career counselling personnel as well as the line manager. But there is a tendency for line managers to neglect their role in this area and to leave it to others. The effects on the individual, their performance, and their colleagues, of the frustration at not having their full potential used, or feeling no incentive to keep developing, can be devastating. Line managers must exercise responsibility for maximising the use of human resources as with any other resource in the company. To ensure continued development, frequent and creative assessment of career possibilities for all staff is essential.

High-flyers generally receive the most attention for career development, but the practice of moving them around the company every six months or so has proved less effective in developing leadership qualities than giving them responsibility early on for a whole section of work that is perceived as being important. The optimum period for maximum development before the next move is about two years.

High-flyers are not always recruited as such, and later developers may 'sprout wings' after a couple of years in the job. A good boss will be sufficiently alert to his or her staff's development to recognise this and provide every opportunity to develop it by giving more responsibility, or broadening experience as part of a promotion preparation plan. Such bosses usually get a reputation for 'growing' the company's best people.

An increasing number of middle and senior managers are described as having 'plateaued' once they have reached the top of the pay scale, have passed 45, and there is no slot in the organisation for them to move up to. The idea that development stops at this stage, that performance tails off and they become partial passengers waiting for early retirement is more of a self-fulfilling prophecy than an inevitability.

It is a waste of human resources to assume that they can make no further contribution. It is because organisations take this attitude, and do not seek ways to continue development or provide new opportunities for further recognition, that the plateaued manager seeks recognition and achievement in activities outside work – thus perpetuating the myth that as far as the company is concerned they are 'spent'. One senior clerk in a transport company had no chance of promotion because his boss was only a year or two older and seemed set there for life, so he progressed through the local golf club and became a very successful and highly respected president, to fulfil his wish for recognition.

The motivation in most jobs tends to fade after four or five years, and if upward mobility is not a possibility, other methods of changing or enriching work must be used to rejuvenate established staff, and give the organisation the longer benefit of their experience and particular skills. For example, additional responsibilities can be given for mentoring a younger protégé from a different department; lateral transfers can open up new and interesting areas of work; and running projects with inter-departmental teams, becoming a trouble-shooter for a wider territory, or researching and developing a new specialism can all recreate incentive to develop. At around 45-55, financial imperatives are often reduced, children have grown up, the mortgage is manageable, and interest, challenge and recognition replace high status and more pay as personal goals for many people.

Career development in the past has always had the connotation of upward movement, but outward career development is just as important, if not more so, in these situations. Organisation development in fast-moving companies that depend on new technologies and rapid change is becoming more organic and less hierarchical. A high-technology fibre manufacturer with a big emphasis on research and fast development of new products has a very shallow structure, with only a few grades to reach senior management, but there is no restraint on the level of responsibility, rewards and recognition other than performance. The innovators and entrepreneurs are not demotivated by the confines of detailed and delimiting job descriptions, nor the boundaries of pay levels. They are rewarded on performance for as long as they perform and meet the challenges that are there. Assessment of performance is thorough and frequent.

Another 'sideways' development activity, even within the restrictions of a hierarchical structure, is training and networking outside the company on exchanges, secondments, shared development programmes, or joint projects. All these activities introduce fresh ideas and new challenges.

Cross-sectoral activity can be particularly rewarding for the company too. A group of blue chip companies has formed a consortium with the civil service and local government to provide a series of intensive one-week courses for senior managers from all sectors. The subjects covered include national and international economic, social and political change of strategic importance, but the greatest value and stimulation is obtained from the mix of perspectives and greater mutual understanding that is achieved.

If you intend to use career planning as a development tool, ask yourself the following questions:

- Do I know my subordinates' aspirations, abilities and potential sufficiently well?
- Do I know enough about career possibilities elsewhere within and outside the organisation?
- Can I enlist the help of the personnel department, professional counselling, or the company trainer to obtain guidance, training, and advice on career development for my subordinates?
- What lateral moves, job enrichment, or other career-widening activities are available for me to use as 're-activators'? How can I create more? Are our job descriptions and pay grades so rigid and limiting that they maintain the minimum and dry up or drive out the motivated with potential? If so, how can I get them changed?

● Had I better start doing all this as quickly as possible and discuss it with my boss before I get caught in the same trap?

Resources
The implications of changing structures on career development are well covered in Career Dynamics: Matching Industrial and Organisational Needs, E. Schein (Addison-Wesley, 1978). This book went out of print in January 2001, but is still a useful resource - check with your library!

25

Use the Trainer

When did you stop ignoring your company trainer? Perhaps you still do, or you may share the view of many managers that the trainers are some kind of witch-doctors who cure the 'problem people' sent to them by muttering magic incantations in the training room. Either way, the common isolation of training units from the mainstream activity of the company is an unnecessary waste of opportunity. Worse, it leaves the frustrated trainer with little else to do but invent jargon and write articles in journals about 'catalysts', 'facilitators' and 'intervention strategies'.

Trainers sometimes bring this upon themselves by creating an air of mystique about training methods, in the mistaken belief that this lends weight to their professional status and credibility. The situation is improving. Many large companies are now disbanding centralised training departments and running their trainers lean and mobile to work alongside managers. Training facilities and in-company courses are still provided, but they are demand-led rather than predetermined by a course programme. Good managers recognise that staff development is their responsibility, but they use all the resources available to them to help them do it effectively.

Trainers have access to expertise, equipment, training materials, information and facilities. See what they have in your organisation and assess what you can use to develop your own people. You could arrange a weekend retreat or immersion course to plan the launching of a new product or to build team commitment in a newly formed working group. If there isn't a training centre suitable to accommodate the group, the trainer can use outside contacts to arrange this and discuss with you the most effective way to achieve what you want out of the session. A great deal of constructive thinking and planning can arise from an intensive period away from the pressures of daily work routines. Colleagues can 'get their jackets off', in the right atmosphere for real communication.

The effect of such a shared experience in welding a group together, and in creating commitment to a mutual objective is very long lasting. But the contributions of the professional trainer to the methods, design and timing of activities, and the briefing of any outside contributors, can be significant in its success. Why not have it as a regular event for your team?

Training is becoming big business and there are as many sharks here as anywhere else. When buying off-the-job training, use your company trainer to investigate what is available and help you to assess what will get you the results you want for your subordinates. They know what is on the market and can read between the lines of the advertising bumph.

You may not need to send people away for training. Discuss with your training people what sessions you want to hold on site, and how you or your staff might participate in the training to keep it relevant to your work schedule. Tips and advice from the trainer might help you and your subordinates to improve your own briefing and coaching techniques too.

Most trainers network with fellow professionals in other organisations and can be a fund of information on staff development techniques elsewhere. They will also know of possibilities for job exchanges and secondment opportunities.

The closer the trainer works with you, the better he or she understands what you are trying to achieve with your team and the more effective the service is to you as a resource. Invite the trainer along regularly to your departmental meetings and team briefings. You should both be aiming for the same objectives, but it is difficult to achieve this unless you share with him your vision of where you are going and how you intend to get there. Effective company trainers need to be as aware of strategic issues as they are of what is happening on the factory floor, and this means working in partnership with all levels of management.

But treat with caution the trainer who meets every problem with the suggestion of a course. Training is not the solution to every problem, and there is a lot more to staff development than courses. People learn best by experience, but only with adequate preparation, coaching and feedback. The trainer can help identify ways of coaching and working that will maximise the development potential of the task. Keep notes on the development you want for each of your subordinates, add to them after appraisal sessions and debriefings, and talk confidentially with the trainer about the best way to achieve it. They will have a view wider than your own department of what has been tried successfully elsewhere.

It is also useful to discuss staff development issues with someone who understands the principles but who is not as close to the problem as you are. A sympathetic outsider can often ask the question which makes you look afresh at situations you have taken for granted.

If you are planning to introduce, for the first time, new systems such as quality circles, action learning sets, project teams or appraisal systems, get the trainer working along with you from the outset. Not only will there be training and development implications in the way these systems are introduced and operated, but training in the appropriate skills will be necessary for those who are going to work the new systems. Many a well-designed staff appraisal scheme has fallen flat on its face and left a wake of discontent and disillusion behind it, simply because those who had to do the appraising had not been trained in essential interpersonal skills. A good boss should be consciously looking for ways of achieving work objectives that will at the same time develop his or her subordinates, but changes in working methods that occur for any other reason are also likely to have potential for development, or to initiate training needs in themselves. It is worth maintaining a close working relation with the company trainer to identify these at an early stage and smooth the path of change.

Last, but far from least, don't forget your own development and training. Whether it is for technical updating, brushing up on your management skills, or joining a mutual problem-solving group of like-minded people from other organisations, a quiet word with the trainer over a pint could give you some valuable ideas and contacts.

With the increasing availability of IT and computers in general, the advances in online training are legion. There are distinct advantages in offering your staff the chance to work through carefully designed programmes which can be completed at their own pace. Of course, you will need the appropriate resources and must also allow time for the training to be completed, but you will not be restricted to only letting your people go on Fridays or when the training department can fit it in. As no two people will learn at exactly the same pace or with the same intensity, online training is ideally placed to meet differing needs, thus allowing all learners to complete courses rather than forcing the slower ones to drop off as the more able ones work faster.

26

Plan Training and Development

When trainers are running a course, the first things they ask the participants are how they came to be on the course and what they expect to get out of it. This is not just to give the trainer time to think, nor idle curiosity. It gives an indication of the participants' motivations and desires.

On any course, there are always two or three who are there because they have been 'sent': they don't know why, or their resentment at the implied criticism prevents them from recognising why, and they don't know what, if anything, they are supposed to do back at base with what they might learn. Ignorance concerning the latter is not really a problem to them, because they are unlikely to learn much anyway.

There are generally others who are there because they always know what courses are on and ask to attend. They are invariably the ones whom their bosses are happiest to release, and they become the professional course attenders. They can even tell the trainer what to do next – and usually do.

A few years ago, the Alfred Marks Group carried out a survey of managers who had been on training courses. Of those interviewed, 67 per cent had not applied what they had learned to their jobs – 23 per cent in fact had made no attempt to do so, and 44 per cent had been unable to because of 'the entrenched attitudes of bosses, company power structure and lack of resources'.

The purpose of training and development is to improve individual and company performance by changing or enhancing behaviour. For this to happen, decisions must be made about what should be taught, how it can be most effectively learned, how to ensure it is applied on the job, and by whom. All these decisions should be made in conjunction with the boss.

Without adequate planning, the wastage of money, skills and time will be added to the frustration of boss and subordinate. This applies to less formal development activities on the job as well as to courses.

Drawing up a training and development plan for your section or depart-ment enables you to ensure that:

- Training/development proposals match the requirements of the business plan and the policy of the organisation.
- The required money and staff time can be budgeted and negotiated.
- Some evaluation of results against plans can be carried out.
- The off-the-job training you want will be available by giving advance notice to your company trainer or other outside providers. You also have time to assess the training on offer and make the best choices.
- You set aside time for coaching, on-the-job instruction or briefing in which you or your staff will be directly engaged.

The first stage is to identify the training and development needs of your employees. Most textbooks will guide you to the job description or suggest you do a job analysis by measuring the difference between required skills/performance and actual skills/performance of the job-holder, and plug the gap. This may be fine for many situations, especially for technical skills, but it implies that training is always remedial, and only for work being done this week, or next month.

Development requires a more positive and further-reaching view. You may wish to increase potential beyond skills being used at the present time, consider job changes in line with development, build up someone's strengths, prepare them for delegation or give them the opportunity for personal development.

The commonly held view that training and development necessarily imply criticism creates a learning block for many employees. Training is always an investment of resources, and whether it is to meet skill deficiencies or enhance potential, it can be seen as a reward and an expression of confidence in the subordinate if you have a positive attitude towards identifying their needs and bring them into the process.

The other standard prescription for training plans is that identification of needs must always precede any training. This is a neat, tidy and logical arrangement, but life is usually none of these things. With employees who are resistant to the idea of development (and this is as common among supervisors who've been in the job for 30 years as it is among senior managers who have been around just as long and don't think they can learn anything), it may be necessary to increase self-awareness by exposing them to planned new experiences and activities (don't call it 'training'), before they will accept the need for further development, or fully appreciate just what is needed. For others, it is often a period of training which realises their potential for further development and perhaps job changes.

Identification and implementation can take place simultaneously. They form a continuous process, whatever your training or management development officer tells you.

When drawing up your training/development plan, it may be useful to consider the following as sources of information or generators of training needs:

Business plan
For example, new products, services, processes, technology, increased targets, changed markets, budgets.

Internal change
Restructuring in own or other departments, mergers, de/re-centralisation, personnel policies, training standards, reorganisations.

External change
Legislation (employment, trading standards, industrial relations); social/economic, professional and technical institute requirements for qualifications or continuing professional development; technical/ professional updating.

Human resource planning
New recruits (induction training), preparation for promotion for retirements or redundancies, changes in jobs, re-skilling, government youth training, and job training schemes.

Organisational policy
Qualification requirements for specific jobs, training leave entitlement, health and safety training.

Individual subordinates
Performance appraisal, coaching, joint discussion on career plans and personal development, job analysis and job description, training requests.

Departmental performance
Complaints, error rates, wastage, performance results (sales, budget, etc.), relations within and between departments.

Your training plan should indicate the reason for the training/ development and who needs/deserves it. The next stage is to determine when, where, how, by whom and how much it will cost. Enlist the co-operation of your company trainer to work out these and the following factors:

- What learning methods best suit the subordinate?
- Will the methods and content be compatible with company/ departmental culture?
- Should the training/development be off-the-job or on-the-job?

You can then complete and cost your plan, and inform others who need to know what your proposals are. There will be some development needs for which you will do the coaching or instructing, and for off-the-job courses you will need to conduct briefing, de-briefing and follow-up reviews if the learning is to be integrated with work effectively. At this point, allow time for these activities in your own work plan over the same period.

Training itself can create training needs. For example, if you have technical, scientific or engineering staff following a qualification course, either by day/block release or distance learning, they are likely to benefit from ancillary training in report-writing and interview skills for oral examination. Anyone following prolonged courses of study for any purpose, especially by open or distance-learning methods, will gain from additional training in study skills, revision and examination techniques – it maintains morale and reduces failure rates. Adult learning needs a lot of encouragement and reinforcement, especially when it is being done part-time - 'students' feel isolated and lose motivation very easily. It helps if contact is made with people in other departments or other organisations who are doing similar courses, and self-help groups are formed for mutual support, or if a mentor is appointed to guide and encourage each student. This should be included in your plan. You need to engage with your 'students' if you have a tutoring role – a real, interactive relationship can greatly benefit you and the learner.

Staff whom you have designated to train others (including yourself), may first need training in coaching and instructional skills. 'Sitting by Nellie' can be a useful form of instruction, but only if Nellie is as competent at passing on her skills as she is at using them.

Subordinates should be consulted when drawing up the departmental training plan, but the final stage is jointly to draw up individual development plans. These record existing qualifications and past training/development experience, current job priorities and future job or promotion proposals if known. Ask subordinates to enter their own development priorities in the short and longer term. After discussion, add your own comments. The last part of the record will contain the agreed training plan, which details courses, exchanges, planned delegation, specific coaching or other experiences and activities, with a time-scale. Both you and the subordinate should have a copy, and it should be updated regularly. An example is given in Figure 26.1.

From your plan you can make a card index of subordinates which indicates what you want to achieve with them in terms of delegation, coaching and other general experience. You can then quickly refer to these when allocating work, or creating other informal opportunities for development.

At an organisational level, training/development plans enable you to ensure you have the right human resources to achieve your business objectives. They are just as important as planning production, re-tooling, or cash flow.

Within the department, they demonstrate your concern for people and their development, provide an environment in which people can reach their full potential, and also let them see realistically the cost and other matters that need to be considered. They will then understand why you sometimes have to say 'no' when they ask to attend a conference, and those who resist development will realise they are missing out on something.

EMPLOYEE DEVELOPMENT PLAN

SECTION A (to be completed by employee)

Name...................... Designation & location ....
....

Date of appointment in present post ....

Description of Works
(Priority areas as you see them)

(Other areas)

Existing qualifications (including any current studies)

Courses, seminars/conferences, exchanges, other formal training activities
in the last 12 months

Your own priorities for your future development
Short term (next 12 months)

Longer term

SECTION B (to be completed after discussion between employee and
supervisor, and/or training officer)

Supervisor's comments

Agreed development plan

Time-scale   Implementation   Dates

Figure 26.1

Resources

Most of the large number of books written on identifying and implementing training needs are aimed at professional trainers, with a great deal of technical detail and jargon (which is one of the reasons why this book was written!). However, many books on general management matters contain sections on training – check out your favourite author.

27

Record Progress

A head of department took part in the selection interview of a young professional two grades below him. The young man got the job despite the senior manager having one or two misgivings about his lack of confidence. The new recruit's immediate superior encouraged his development by delegation and coaching, and 18 months later proposed him for upgrading in line with company policy. The head of department resisted this on the grounds that the young man lacked confidence and experience, though he had never actually seen him in operation; in fact he had hardly seen him at all in the intervening period, and was still judging him on the first impressions of his interview!

People change and develop, some faster than others, depending on their natural aptitude and the way they are managed. It is essential that those responsible for making decisions about their future are well informed on progress. Change can be overlooked either because we are too distant from people or too close to them to recognise their growth. We have a fixed image in our minds as to what Alice or Jack is like and what they are capable of, and we don't take time to stand back, review, and adjust it. People can be completely turned off work when they realise their development has not been registered and they are being held down as a result.

Maintaining records of achievement and progress helps us to keep our perceptions of staff up to date. It also enables them to see for themselves how they have developed and encourages them to feel responsible for further self-development. They can feel a sense of pride in how far they have come, consider the direction in which they want to develop, and determine the means of getting there with our support. Records provide bench-marks to reflect upon as well as to plan for the future.

There are various methods of recording progress; the important thing is that the subordinate should also have a copy, or better still, a record of his or her own. Record-keeping should obey the following principles:

● Where performance can clearly be credited to an individual (e.g. sales,

121

output, turn-around time, etc.), a record of targets and best performance should be kept and due recognition as well as note be taken of when best results are overtaken by even better ones.

- Individual training/development plans provide a record of courses and planned development activities which help to build up a picture of a subordinate's growth, and joint discussion for up-dating both jogs your memory and lets them know you are up to date on their progress.

- Key tasks or goals to be achieved over a set period should be written down somewhere in such a way that their achievement can also be recorded, and whether performance exceeded expectations, e.g. within budget and before the deadline. Where subordinates work in teams and specific allocation of performance results is difficult, it is even more important that their own share in team achievement is recognised and seen in black and white.

- Regular appraisal, whether a formally documented system or not, should produce written conclusions on assessment and future action, of which the subordinate retains a copy. This is a good occasion to discuss and record such personal development as improvements in influencing skills, confidence, accepting responsibility, or interpersonal skills.

- When subordinates go on courses, exchanges, projects and other off-the-job development activities, written summaries should be kept of the pre-briefing, debriefing and review interviews for you both to look back on, not only to record subordinates' progress through these experiences, but to recall those which were most effective for learning and for application to the job.

- Subordinates can be asked to submit regular progress reports on their key tasks. These should be brief (no more than one side of A4) and they should be read, and preferably commented upon, by you so that the writers are assured their reports are not just entering an abyss. Reports have the advantage that subordinates are encouraged to identify what they see as their key achievements, but beware – ignored progress reports are very counter-productive!

All these methods are also suitable for up-dating your boss, or your boss's boss, on the progress of your subordinates, and could help when negotiating for upgradings, promotions, or justifying your training budget. They will also demonstrate how well you manage and develop your staff.

Another effective method of recording progress, but for the reference and development of the individual not for management, is to encourage your staff to maintain their own personal development files. These can contain their copies of appraisal interview notes, course pre-briefings and debriefings, their own training/development plans, their personal goals and achievements, notes on things they want to discuss with you about their future, information on courses and other development possibilities, and their performance results.

These are their own personal files (there is no reason why you should not have one for yourself too). It encourages responsibility for self-development, gives them written evidence of progress to look through, and provides the expectations that they will have the opportunity to go on from where they are for as far as they are able.

Give some recognition and ceremony to the idea by presenting for this purpose a really smart, hard-backed file with their initials embossed, to each of your team, and to new recruits during their induction.

28

Integrate Off-the-job Training

Most of this book is about your role as a boss in developing the people who work for you (or with you), by the way you manage them, the work, and yourself day by day. But there are occasions when training or development is best achieved by a period spent away from the workplace, whether this is for technical skill training and up-dating, educational or professional qualifications, or behavioural development such as interpersonal skills which may need a supportive environment away from personal risk.

Whether the absence from work is a day or several months, the greatest difficulty with such training is making the transfer from what is learned at the time to what is subsequently practised in the workplace, and your role is crucial in enabling this to happen so that you get the results you and your employees want from the experience and the investment. However keen the learner or competent the trainer, the boss can make or break the value of off-the-job training and development for subordinates and the organisation.

You will have the greatest responsibility in this process for those who report directly to you, but it extends all the way down the line. By setting the right example with your immediate subordinates you can encourage them to do the same for the people who report to them.

Many bosses feel threatened by bright young stars in their departments learning new skills and perhaps knowing something they don't. The best way to turn this threat into a strength is to manage their newly acquired abilities in achieving your objectives as you would with any new or enhanced resource. The other way is to make sure you keep learning a few new tricks yourself.

The effective management of off-the-job training and development requires bringing the boss into your plans before, during, and after the training period, and developing a partnership approach with the training providers as well as those undergoing the training or development. There are six steps that ensure this process takes place:

1. Identify the need

Whether or not there is a training manager in the organisation, the identification of training and development needs should also be carried out by the boss and the subordinate. Chapter 26 details common generators of training needs and other sources of information in assessing them. However the need has arisen, both you and your subordinate should be quite clear as to why the training is necessary and what contribution you expect it to make to the performance of the individual and the section or department.

But remember that poor performance does not in itself indicate a training need unless you know exactly what is causing it. Training cannot remotivate a disillusioned employee. On the contrary, lack of motivation might indicate a training need for the boss.

2. Decide on the method

Whether the training provider is likely to be a business school, a technical college, university, skills centre, an online training supplier, or the organisation's own training department, there is a range of options for most needs. It may be that a short secondment or temporary transfer would achieve the objectives better than a course anyway. But if a course is required, don't just use the nearest, or fill in the booking form in the latest advertising that has landed on your desk. Don't even use your own company's training staff unless you are certain that the content and method are suitable for what you want and for the individual concerned. Find out who offers the training you're looking for. Go and have a look at the place, see what they are doing and ask them to put you in touch with previous clients, and then speak to the clients they did not tell you about.

Beware of picking the shortest because it is cheaper. Learning is not always a fast business, particularly where behavioural skills are concerned. Such skills need time for reflection, practice and reinforcement. Whatever the advertising says, no one is going to return overflowing with human understanding and the ability to motivate staff after a three-day course – however good the hotel was! Obviously too, the person attending the course should have a say in the selection if you want to get him or her fully committed at the outset.

3. The pre-briefing

About a week before the training or development experience, sit down for a few minutes with the person who is attending it and reinforce the reasons for going, what you hope he or she will get out of it, and what will be expected on their return. The expectations should be specific and to an agreed time schedule, e.g. measurable standard of performance, briefing to the rest of the team within so many weeks, a full report to you or other interested parties by a certain date, or a specific project to be undertaken.

4. Participation during training

The extent to which this is useful depends on the type and length of training. For in-company induction courses or skills training in which you have particular expertise, there is value in participating formally or informally by pre-arrangement with the training staff. For external courses, or those concerned with personal and behavioural development, it is better to leave people to make their own relationships in a new and different environment without the boss breathing down their necks. For long college-based training, distance day/block release or off-site, online training, regular reinforcement of goals and discussion on progress is essential.

There may be critical stages at which some personal coaching from you, or someone else in the company could get the student over a difficult hurdle. This needs to be done before it jeopardises his or her performance. Students may be reluctant to say they are in trouble; maintaining contact and good listening skills will tell you when they are, and it could save you a lot of time and money.

If you receive a progress or performance report on your subordinates, always share it with them, and let them comment first. If the report is good, your praise and recognition will encourage even greater effort. If it is bad, the problem can only be solved by working at it together on agreed action.

5. The debriefing

This should take place as soon as possible after completion of training and should be high enough on your priority list to ensure that it does. Let your subordinates tell you what they have done and how they think they can use it to achieve the goals that were agreed. Listen for what they have learned and what they need next, then draw up a joint action plan which covers the following:

- When, where, how and to whom they will give a briefing or report on the course for the benefit of others in the team.
- Opportunities in the next few days/weeks for practising the skills or knowledge learned, with feedback and coaching from you.
- A work plan for the next few months, incorporating what has been learned and extending it where appropriate.
- An agreed date for a review of the whole exercise in, say, 6 months.

6. Review

This is the time to judge the return on your investment and to reinforce yet again your continued interest in performance after training. If company training staff have conducted the training, get them in on the review discussion too; they should be delighted at the opportunity for follow-up evaluation. At this stage, you will need to assess whether further training is necessary in the near future, or more experience, perhaps in a different section or even a different organisation, would be better. It is a good time for a general appraisal of both the job and the subordinate, and to update their work, training, and development plan for the next 12 months.

All this may seen a lot on first reading. But it is basically about attitude rather than about time. For the boss who puts regular face-to-face contact with subordinates high on the priority list, and already knows the personalities and capabilities of his staff, the extra attention required to integrate off-the-job training is little compared to the costs of course fees and lost production time.

29

Learn to Instruct

The notion of manager as trainer is gaining credibility for sound business reasons. For training to have a direct impact upon performance, it needs to be as closely linked to real work as possible. This includes time, place, receptiveness of those being trained and the relevance of what is being taught. The right time for your section and the things you wish to teach may be just before the back shift, before the store opens, when a new consignment arrives, as soon as there is a trough in the workload, or when the rain stops.

If you're doing the training, it can be on your own equipment and in your own environment, and can include both recipients and their supervisors; and you will be a participant in their learning experience. All except the last point can probably be met by having an instructor come into your workplace by prior arrangement, but there will be occasions when your knowledge of the employees, of the subject matter and of the goals you are working towards make you the best person to do the training.

This whole book is about you, the manager, as trainer and developer, but straight instruction is different from other forms of development. Coaching, for example, is based on joint problem-solving and giving guidance rather than just providing the answers. People develop better if they are in charge of their own learning. But there are situations when more formal instruction is the most appropriate method of learning, e.g. giving information or knowledge about changes in procedures, legislation or methods of work, new products/service details, passing on technical skills, or introducing someone to a new job/task for the first time.

Although instruction is more formal and directive than, say, coaching, it should not be a totally one-way, authoritarian tirade, like a sergeant-major taking drill or loading a rifle by numbers. There should be as much opportunity for participation and practice as possible.

Whether the instruction is on a one-to-one basis or to a group (in the form of a talk), or teaching a practical skill, the following checklists for action before, and during instruction may be useful.

Preparation for instruction

Reflect on the person or people you are going to instruct and determine the right pace and level for their existing knowledge, experience and intellectual ability. Don't fall into the trap of some further-education teachers who confuse lack of knowledge with lack of intelligence and instruct everyone in words of one syllable – the 'trainee' may have a higher IQ than you. On the other hand, don't talk over people's heads to show how well you know the subject – concentrate instead on showing how well you can instruct!

Bone up on the job or the subject matter being taught, especially if it is some time since you have been concerned with it. Prepare the session carefully; don't take your experience and knowledge for granted. Your subordinates will learn better from a logical sequence, not just how things come to you at the time. Be clear on exactly what the recipients need to know or be able to do and to what standard, and how you and they are going to measure it, and know when they've got there. Run through the sequences in your mind – or even better, with a tame audience, such as a long-suffering partner – to be sure that you are making sense.

Check out any computers, equipment or machinery to be used, whether for the practice of the trainee or for your own visual aids. A course on how to make video training films once began with a suitably brief introduction before we all got our hands on a camera – unfortunately for the instructor, nothing worked because he had hired incompatible systems.

Check out the time and place for instruction. Is it next door to machines, canteen or other places likely to be noisy at the time you want to use it? Are you going to be interrupted by telephones, tea trolleys, or the MD looking for a quiet smoke? Set aside sufficient time – not just for your bit, but to allow subordinates to ask questions or practise under your supervision.

Giving instruction

Adults under instruction are usually nervous because of fear of failure, and anxiety about the unknown. Reduce uncertainty as early as possible by outlining what you and they are going to do. The old army instructor's motto is useful to remember: 'Tell 'em what you're going to tell 'em; tell 'em; then tell 'em what you told 'em'.

For practical one-to-one instruction, the method should be based on the sequence 'tell-show-do' - explain the methods and standards required, demonstrate what you have said, and let them have a go themselves while you give feedback. Hands-on experience should be given as early as possible, e.g. in computer training or the use of measuring instruments.

Check understanding frequently by asking questions, or getting them to demonstrate on equipment. Allow plenty of opportunities for their questions, preferably as you go along rather than at the end – if you are sufficiently well prepared, this should not disturb your planned sequence of instruction. Above all, be patient.

Make the teaching as close to real work as possible, e.g. train for required standards and speeds on the job rather than reduced levels for training purposes, otherwise they will have to learn it over again at another level. Set the skills or information being taught in the context of their jobs, the department, the organisation, wherever possible.

Record progress and share it with those you are instructing. Knowing how they are doing is part of the learning process.

Don't drop people in the deep end too soon. Apart from mistakes which you may not find acceptable, uncertainty and failure negate learning and the desire to learn. Be on hand for feedback and follow-up. Treat initial mistakes as learning opportunities without making people feel small, and they will admit errors and learn from them rather than hide them.

Provide brief handouts covering the main teaching points, reference diagrams, or essential instructions (e.g. safety). If instruction is about new procedures, products, marketing or working methods etc., always have examples to use during instruction, and to leave with them if appropriate.

Enthuse – it is motivating and highly infectious.

A chat with your company trainer on techniques, materials and equipment may well be fruitful. He or she might also offer further advice on methods to use if those you want to instruct are widely dispersed and you don't want to bring them into the centre every time you want to give instruction. Computer-based training, online training and tele-conferencing, for example, can be useful in the right situation.

A sideways thought: if your organisation uses 'sitting by Nellie' as a standard method for staff training or induction, how much more effective and confident Nellie would be, if she too had the benefit of some training in instruction skills.

As usual, there are spin-offs for you in learning how to instruct your staff. Teaching is one of the best ways to sharpen up one's own perception of a subject, and you will learn a lot about your employees and their learning and development needs for future reference.

Resources

See *Teacher, Trainer, Tutor* by Liz O'Rourke, for some excellent advice about creating a good working relationship with your 'students'. Management Books 2000, 2001.

30

Use Visual Aids to Communicate

Visual aids are just that: things to look at which help people to understand and retain what they are being told. Even the most intelligent retain only a fraction of what they hear. Our minds are so busy receiving signals from other senses about all sorts of things we may not be aware of consciously, that most of what we are told simply gets lost under the brain's enormous work-load. If what we hear is accompanied at the same time by appropriate visual signals, retention is doubled. If the message can engage all our senses – sound, sight, touch, smell and taste – then the chances of the message being understood and retained are at their maximum. Using more than one sense simultaneously to grab attention is part of the success of television advertising, and why the stallholder invites you to feel the cloth, or taste the cheese.

This fact is used not only by salesmen, teachers and trainers, but was on one occasion used to good effect by ratepayers to speed the process of decision-making. A local town council had been dragging its feet over filling in a shallow stagnant pond on which an elderly lady kept a few ducks. The local residents complained to the council when rats began to invade the neighbourhood. When nothing was done for several months, the incensed ratepayers attended the next council meeting accompanied by a cage full of rats which they let loose among the councillors to get their point across. They did so with profound success.

More conventional visual aids are used increasingly in council chambers, boardrooms and cabinet offices to inform and get ideas accepted. Why let people in those places have all the fun? If visual aids increase understanding, impact and commitment, why not use them to get your message across to your own team?

This chapter describes a few simple hints for using visual aids effectively that can improve your confidence and image not only in giving team briefings, but in presenting your ideas to the boss or in making public speeches.

Visual aids vary in complexity of use, cost and preparation time, but whatever the medium you choose, the golden rule for any presentation is to approach your audience with a KISS – Keep It Simple Stupid! It is more effective to get one or two key ideas across clearly and briefly than to spend half an hour on convoluted instruction, with numerous points and elaborate illustrations.

Visual aids enhance a presentation; but they cannot rescue a poor communicator. Indeed, used without sufficient planning and practice, they can demolish the most expert orator. But once you have mastered them, you can increase the confidence and communication skills of your staff by coaching and encouraging them in the same techniques. It will improve the quality and efficiency of the way they pass information to you and to each other. The variety of visual aids is considerable – we will start with the simplest.

- Use **flip charts** for brainstorming, building up graphs, budget statements, etc., during briefings and formal presentations. Check your writing can be read at the back of the room and ensure the pad is firmly fixed. Striding up with pen poised over the pad only to have it fall in a heap at your feet is more amusing for the audience than the speaker.

- **White boards** are just as quick and easy to use, and there are now sophisticated models which print out on the spot any number of paper copies of what is written on the board. It's expensive, but might impress customers and members of the board. Don't use indelible or spirit-based pens – what you write will not wipe off! There are few more deflating experiences than to write your first cryptic point with a flourish, then find you can't clean it off to make way for the pièce de résistance.

- Overhead projectors are useful because no blacking out is necessary and transparencies can be made on a PC to a high standard. Any printed material can be copied on to transparencies. For the greatest impact, images should be bold and colourful – use cartoons, humour and symbolism, which are great communicators. Draw your own, or identify one of your staff who can draw and encourage them to develop their talents, or make useful contacts with your public relations or training departments. A little preparation is time well spent with any visual aids. Your words of wisdom are likely to evaporate when you switch on the OHP and find your progress chart is upside down. Finally, always have a spare bulb – and know how to fit it!

- Photographic slides and video film need more forward planning and preparation of course, but can have a lot of impact. It can develop a perceptive and critical eye in your staff if they participate in producing them. Get them to take slides, or video clips of site works, new projects, good and bad practices, the behaviour of customers, or any other aspect of your business or service. The results can be used for team discussion, induction for new recruits, or demonstrating progress to your boss or the board of directors.

- Several ranges of ready-made training videos are available for informal training sessions in your own unit when it suits you. John Cleese has made a whole series which are not only very funny but thought provoking, e.g. on time management and effective meetings.

- There are several very effective computer-based presentation systems which allow you to present material on anything from a laptop to a projection screen for larger meetings. Use a staff member with good design skills or hire an external expert to help you create the presentation. Most programs come with self-help instructions and prepared blank frames. You can create very effective presentations with professional-looking fades and other visual effects quite simply. Remember that most people now are very familiar with sophisticated television and video programmes and advertising, so you must show them something that is not too rough or amateurish.

If your organisation has a training department, take time to go and look at the equipment and resources there. Try them out and become familiar with them before you decide what suits you best.

Visual aids can of course be very simple indeed and may consist of a single exhibit. If you want to read the riot act to your team about a piece of shoddy production, or rubbish around the work area, bring it in, put in on the table and let them see, touch, and smell it too!

But visual aids don't always have to be brought into the office or the briefing room. Take employees to look at a project or see a new product, to watch customer behaviour, talk to clients, sit in on a meeting – actually experience with all their senses the message you want to get over. Briefings or training sessions before and after the field experience can clarify the message and check understanding. Whenever it is important to put across a message to your team, ask yourself how many of their senses you can bring into the process – it's more fun that way, and it's also more effective.

31

Brief Your Team

'Meetings, Bloody Meetings!' - the heartfelt cry of the busy manager – expresses such a widespread problem that John Cleese made a very successful training film with that title. His judgement was sound because he had to meet the enormous demand with a sequel, 'More Bloody Meetings'.

We all know the professional 'committee' people who can never be found because they are always at some meeting, or those who call meetings at the slightest provocation because they get an ego-trip out of lording it in the chair. For them, rushing indispensably from venue to venue satisfies their need for activity without actually having to do anything.

There is no point in having a meeting just for the sake of gathering. There has to be a purpose which can only be fulfilled by the face-to-face contact of a specific group of participants. When it comes to meetings with your own subordinates, they have the dual purpose of developing your staff as well as exchanging information.

The term 'team briefing' has been taken over to mean semi-official meetings to pass down a brief containing information on company policy and activities which has been drawn up usually by the head of the organisation. That is not what this chapter is about. It is about informal meetings which you have with your subordinates to discuss matters of mutual importance in achieving your goals. These may on occasion include items on company policy, but it is you who decides the agenda, i.e. you as the leader not as a company messenger.

Effective leaders have to balance the attention they give to:

- the **task**: making deadlines, selecting priorities, getting resources, measuring results
- the **individual**: gaining commitment, developing/training, caring for the whole person
- the **team**: encouraging cohesion, matching talents, establishing common goals and mutual support.

Concentrating solely on the needs of the task and ignoring the people soon loses their commitment and sense of purpose. Developing working relationships only on a one-to-one basis can result in the isolation of your subordinates from each other and destructive competitiveness between them. Specific attention must be given to welding the team together so that they operate effectively on delegated tasks, and potentiate each other's abilities. Regular team briefings are a useful way of achieving the following:

- sharing information
- clarifying and reinforcing goals
- sparking off ideas
- forming deeper relationships within the team
- enabling you to see the team in operation and assessing how well people are working together.

Team briefings can be held at any time when there is something specific to be discussed – some new equipment, a big order, changes in procedures. But there is value in having a short meeting every week on a set day and time. Depending how much has to be covered, they may run for 15 or 30 minutes, but should rarely go beyond this. There is a spin-off in time management when everyone knows there will be an opportunity to discuss things regularly; it reduces the number of ad hoc interruptions for you and your subordinates, for any non-immediate queries can be saved for the briefing when everyone is there.

Careful thought should go into choosing the best day and time. The leader of an architectural design team chose 9.00 am prompt on Monday mornings and runs his meetings for no more than 20 minutes. Apart from ensuring everyone arrives at work on time, it gives a purposeful start to the week. Like himself, most team members have ideas and thoughts on current projects over the weekend and it gives a chance to air them before the demands of routine work take over. The briefings usually start with a little jovial banter about the weekend, which also helps to break through the pain barrier of Monday mornings!

An editor in a large publishing firm used to hold his weekly briefings on Friday afternoons with a bottle of wine. Serious business was discussed, but the meetings were more important as reflective exercises and confirmation of team spirit by sharing the experiences of the week. They often spilled over into the local hostelry afterwards.

When you run your briefings, have an agenda, but give the team ample time to ask questions and raise points themselves. Tell them also about the work you are doing which has a direct bearing on them, and the rest of the section or department. You can use the opportunity to get ideas from them on issues you will have to deal with in the near future, and follow through by reporting progress at the next briefing. This reinforces the feeling that you and they are working for the same goals, and stimulates them to contribute more by giving them a broader perspective.

Don't do all the talking. Make it an opportunity to listen to how the team is working, and to pick up needs and ideas as they arise. 'Yes, Julie, that sounds a really good idea, why don't you and Stan have a detailed look at it and we'll talk about it at the next briefing.' But any promises you make about taking action on their behalf, or letting them follow up a project, should be realistic, because they must be kept. Team briefings build up loyalty and trust but they also make the lack of them more visible.

You can increase the development value of briefings by asking different team members to chair the meeting sometimes. Be sure everyone gets a turn and look out for training needs in communication skills, briefing techniques and verbal presentation. Don't criticise at the meeting, but give feedback afterwards; if necessary arrange a course followed by practice and coaching and see how well they do next time.

If there is really nothing for a briefing agenda, use the time to have a brainstorming session. It may produce some creative ideas as well as promoting a lot of fun and group feeling. Knowing there is a regular meeting develops creativity anyway. People think more about their work because they want to contribute something worthwhile when they get the chance.

Don't restrict yourself to briefings of your immediate subordinates. Go along to the briefings they hold for their own staff. The same development opportunities exist there, but in that situation you won't be in the chair – unless invited to do so, and it would be better to decline. Always let your subordinate know in advance that you are looking in on his or her briefing session and tell them of anything you intend to raise there. Your main role in a subordinate's briefing is to listen and support. After the meeting, give feed-back to your subordinate in private on how he or she handled it.

Regular briefings where everyone can ask questions will sometimes put you on the spot. If you don't know the answer to a question, don't bluff; say so, find out, and tell them later. The same goes for admitting your mistakes. Your team doesn't want to be blinded by your halo, they want to see a human being they can identify with and respect – for your weaknesses as well as strengths. Briefings help them to know and respect you better too.

Resources

To take team briefings further and use them as an opportunity for team development, consult the following book – Team Development Manual, Mike Woodcock (Gower) - which includes activities and exercises you can use.

32

Keep Up To Date

We live in a fast-moving society where change is occurring at an increasing and totally unprecedented rate. New technologies enable products to develop and come on to the market in a fraction of the time it took less than a lifetime ago.

Vacuum cleaners and refrigerators developed in the United States in the early 1900s took 34 years to come to the sales counter. The postwar development of television and spindriers took only 8 years. In particularly volatile industries, such as electronics, it used to take 6 months, but the discovery of the micro-chip rocked the Swiss watch industry overnight. The bad news about development and progress is that if you're not in amongst it, you get left behind in a big way.

The huge advances in technology and IT in particular mean that any organisation has to keep a good weather eye on changes that might affect the way it operates. Communication between organisations and individuals is now virtually instant and the 'micro-isation' of the associated technology offers opportunities for complete changes in working practices. Keeping up to date with professional and technological change is an essential part of staff development if your subordinates are to be able to contribute positively to change and improvement in their own sphere of work, and in the organisation as a whole, whether they are computer engineers, designers, sales people, production workers, or teachers.

It is easy to get bogged down with current workload and never have time to see what is going on around you. The danger is that sooner or later you discover the hard way that nobody wants what you've been working away at anymore because it's been overtaken, or there are new and better ways to do it.

Part of your role as leader is to ensure that staff have the opportunity for up-dating. Share it with them as a priority. Encourage them to be more than just 'fire-fighters'; they might even discover a better extinguisher!

Take out corporate subscriptions to a good range of technical, professional and management journals – and resist the temptation to hang on to them yourself. If you find an especially good one, get more than one copy so that they circulate quickly, and ask someone to set up a proper circulation and chase-up system, with eventual storage at a central resource point.

You could set up a rota for individuals to summarise particularly relevant articles and distribute copies of their notes to their colleagues and yourself. This will develop study and communication skills and is a good exercise for the kind of person who rushes around doing things all day, and rarely takes the time for reflection and thought. It also encourages the responsibility to share important technical data with colleagues – fostering a team approach.

If one of your staff shows a special interest in a new development, enable him or her to have time to follow it through with further research. There should be an end product, such as a report on how their results might be applied to their work.

Delegate to a small team the responsibility for setting up a resource library in your section. Allocate them a budget, and let them scan current material, liaise with colleagues, and determine their own acquisition policy. There may be other collections of data elsewhere in the organisation. Suggest they network with other sections in arranging mutual access and joint purchases of more expensive materials.

Review what access you or your boss might have to other sources of data, such as specialist committees in professional institutes, or technical working parties. Where possible, share this with your team or make it available to their resource library.

Encourage people to take up membership of professional and technical institutes and societies. Even if they are not yet qualified, associate or student membership usually gives access to central libraries and other sources of information. Your company's corporate membership should enable large numbers of employees to benefit from facilities.

Most forward-looking professional institutes as well as other organisations have started a policy of Continuing Professional Development (CPD), and have made it a requirement that their members undertake a specified number of hours' training and development each year. This need not imply formal courses. It can include project work, seminars, individual study, and research. Give your staff the facilities and a set amount of time each month to plan a programme of CPD activities as a team. Suggest ways in which existing projects could contribute to their development programme. Participate in their monthly training sessions by giving presentations from time to time. Find out what the company training officer can do to facilitate your staff's CPD programme, perhaps through training contacts in other organisations.

Look out for seminars, exhibitions and conferences, and ensure that a fair distribution of employees attend, instead of the few who always seem to know what is on and have time to go – the professional conference attenders. It is often more effective to send more than one person, so that they can compare notes and potentiate each other's benefit from the experience.

Afterwards, ask them to present a verbal and/or written report for the benefit of yourself and their colleagues at the next briefing meeting, or at a special meeting if it is important enough.

If you establish efficient ways of enabling employees to remain up to date, and make it a priority by allocating adequate time and money to it, you will be developing them in numerous ways, but you will also find that they keep you up to date too with the minimum of effort on your part. With the time you save, you could take out a subscription to a couple of good training journals and keep yourself informed on what training and development methods other organisations are using effectively.

32

Encourage Mutual Support

Friendly competition between subordinates can be a spur to effort and development if it is open competition, i.e. everyone has a chance to win in return for the required effort, and the target is realistic. It can add spice to work but like any other spice must be used sparingly and with care, or conflict could be the result, and the goal will become personal one-upmanship rather than consistent achievement for the whole team.

Too much competition can exacerbate situations which have a potential for conflict. There are many, but the following are common. Do they exist in your department?

- Unclear or overlapping functional boundaries may lead to power struggles and conflict over work territory.
- Unclear goals can lead to disputes over direction, as well as the means of getting there.
- Insufficient resources, lack of understanding of their means of allocation, or unfair distribution may result in wasteful wrangles over who gets what.
- If values are not made clear and are not shared and regularly reinforced, conflict may arise over determining standards and priorities.
- Ambiguity in performance measurement may lead to disputes over levels of reward and comparability of workloads.
- Incompatible personalities can create havoc and also bring out latent conflict in any of the situations above. But personality clashes are more often the symptom of other underlying causes of conflict than the only cause. Problems may unexpectedly recur after the departure of the 'trouble-maker'.
- Poor communications can result in uncertainty, gossip and misinformation.

It is not possible to eliminate conflict; it seems to be part of the human condition. Managed effectively, it can even have advantages, such as bringing chronic problems into the open, creating the energy to work through difficult issues, clearing the air to make way for better understanding, and stimulating articulate debate on a point of disagreement.

But these advantages only accrue if the conflict is managed in the early stages. Potential conflict that is not recognised and handled positively when the symptoms first appear can be destructive, and completely displace the objectives of the workplace.

Staff development is particularly vulnerable to the destructive effects of conflict, because it depends on good working relationships, and an atmosphere of trust and sharing between subordinates as well as between subordinates and their boss. Once uncertainty, suspicion, and 'taking sides' intervene in relationships, everyone is too preoccupied watching the space between their shoulder blades to seek out opportunities for developing their own skills and those of others around them.

To maintain a mutually supportive atmosphere which encourages development and makes destructive conflict less likely, manage conflict for positive results as early as possible. Create a working environment in which mutual support is openly valued.

Managing conflict positively requires a detailed understanding of your team and the work they do so that you can be aware of latent conflict and recognise its expression at the earliest opportunity. It also requires good communication and interpersonal skills – whatever the cause.

But don't attempt to rush in and solve every dispute that erupts between your employees. You may have to begin the process by counselling the disputants, but they will learn better how to resolve their own differences and achieve greater mutual understanding if you suggest ways in which they could handle the situation, rather than giving a summary arbitration. Imposed solutions invariably leave at least one loser, who will be a latent source of conflict for the future.

If there is disagreement on the best solution to a design problem, for example, rather than let your staff become increasingly entrenched in justifying their opposing views, suggest they go back to the point where there is agreement, i.e. to the original brief. Get them to re-examine the problem it poses, and to restate it. By returning to a shared goal, and looking at it from a different viewpoint, they are more likely to find a course of action upon which both can agree – and it will probably be a better one than the pet solutions they had each latched on to in the first place. There is great potential for development in this situation for both better problem-solving and more effective interpersonal skills.

Where conflict arises from external forces beyond your control, share the problem as far as possible with your team, and, with their full participation, focus on goals which are not in dispute. Reduce uncertainty with accurate information, and concentrate on building team solidarity around areas of agreement.

Where disputes arise from functional boundaries, work allocation, rewards, or standards – with or without the added flavour of personality differences – the solution likely to be both effective and developmental is one in which the disputants share the decision-making and the subsequent action, e.g. in drawing up and monitoring work standards, in determining the equitable distribution of work, or rearranging the membership of specific work groups. There is greater commitment to the solution when people are clear on the goals, can see how the conflict is preventing their achievement, and are expected to contribute to resolving it themselves with your guidance.

The aim is not to leave anyone as a loser, but to get to a situation where everyone can win something. This must be a long-term solution which tackles the root cause of the conflict. Buying-off opposition may lead to short-term agreement, but if it only subdues symptoms, the ameliorative effects will soon wear off and the underlying cause will result in further conflict expressed in the same or different ways.

The positive management of conflict does in itself contribute to the creation of a mutually supportive environment where destructive conflict is less likely to occur. It establishes an atmosphere of trust by demonstrating that differences can and will be resolved beneficially. It becomes easier to bring disputes into the open, and to talk about them before the problem itself gets buried in acrimony.

The key skill is the ability to communicate effectively. This includes being aware of the powerful influence which attitudes and feelings have on behaviour. When these are not known, we tend to make our own assumptions and act accordingly – often incorrectly.

> George was a farmer whose tractor broke down in the middle of the ploughing season. He was despondent because the weather was about to break, but being staunchly independent, he hated asking others for help. Eventually his wife persuaded him to ask their neighbour, Bob, if he could borrow his tractor. George went reluctantly, and all the way along the winding track to Bob's farm he went over in his mind how the conversation would go. 'Bob will ask why I want to borrow his tractor; when I say mine's broken, he'll ask what if I break his too; then I'll say well, I'd mend it; but he'll ask why I don't mend mine; if I say I'm in a hurry while the weather holds, he'll say so is he ...' All this went back and forth through George's mind while he walked, and when he finally reached his neighbour's house, and Bob opened the door, George glanced up and said, 'Stick your bloody tractor, then!' and stalked off.

People's problems have the added dimension that information on attitudes and feelings, which are essential to understanding, remain 'hidden' unless they are sought. People need encouragement to make clear their view of things so that mutual understanding is achieved. This in itself will often resolve what appear to be real conflict when in fact there is none. Here are some ways to proceed:

- Listen to your staff, and encourage them to listen to each other so that effective communication is maintained.
- Create opportunities at meetings and briefings to discuss how people feel about work and relationships, as well as hard data on progress and budgeting.
- Discourage subordinates from jumping to conclusions when things go wrong and others seem guilty – be an example yourself by asking and listening before making assumptions where people are concerned.
- Create opportunities for people to assist each other, e.g. delegate work to small groups or pairs, as well as to individuals.
- Establish a system of mentoring within your own department.
- Appoint sponsors to assist new recruits to pick up both the work and the informal networks.
- Train subordinates to coach each other according to their own particular strengths.
- Encourage people to counsel each other on personal or work problems when appropriate.

Be aware too of the balance between contact time spent with individuals as opposed to groups, or the whole team. One-to-one contact is important in getting to know someone but, if this is the predominant method of contact, you may inadvertently be discouraging them from thinking and acting as a team, and therefore learning to give each other support.

If your subordinates tend to work on individual projects, ensure that they meet regularly as a group to discuss wider issues. If you work on a team basis, give stronger recognition to group identity by having team names, for example, or mascots.

Subordinates can be a powerful influence for developing each other if conflict is managed, and mutual support encouraged. 'Divide and rule' oppresses rather than develops.

34

Socialise

All of us enjoy getting right away from work and all its associations and contacts from time to time, but unfortunately our little escapes don't always work according to plan.

> One senior manager had had a tough day; the perennial personality clash with his counterpart in another department was taking on the nature of a running battle and had come to a head. Looking forward to a pleasant diversion, he took his wife to a private charity concert in a local mansion – one of those intimate occasions which include buffet and drinks after the performance. Having gone off to refill glasses, he was horrified to find on his return that his wife and that of his workplace opponent were in close and jolly conversation. They had been wives of the same organisation for years but were either oblivious to or not interested in their husbands' relations with each other. The two senior managers were forced to spend the remainder of the evening in cool politeness on the periphery of their wives' voluble conviviality.

In small communities, or in lines of business where professional and social circles tend to intersect, it can be difficult to sort out the right relationship for the occasion without, for example, feeling taken advantage of at work because of obligations and contacts outside, or vice versa. It can be even more difficult when dealing with subordinates and particularly in demonstrating fairness in applying standards, rewards and discipline, for example. There are inherent dangers in being too chummy at the bar one day, and having to carry out an objective appraisal interview the next.

Many managers avoid the problem by remaining aloof from their staff at work, and gain the reputation for being cold and withdrawn. You don't have to seek popularity, or be 'one of the lads', but human enough to enable your staff to relate to you as a person, and for you to be sufficiently acquainted with them to know who it is you are managing, and how best to develop them. It won't work if your office becomes a hermitage, and your desk a refuge from which communications emanate only in paper chains and disembodied telephone conversations.

There has to be a certain distance between the boss and his or her subordinates because a leader stands out and is someone who is respected, and entrusted to give direction and to take responsibility for it; but it is a fine line, established through exercising the qualities of leadership while maintaining close working relationships with others. It is an extremely difficult balance to achieve and there are no set rules or magic formulae.

But without this equilibrium between close, mutual understanding and the distance which comes from being authoritative (not authoritarian), management of people becomes difficult, and staff development almost impossible. Consider the effects and advantages of socialisation:

- Getting others to share your values and attitudes towards the job can only be done by regular face-to-face contact; your team needs to get close enough to you to know what you stand for.
- Informal friendly contact aids socialisation, by which people learn the desired behaviours at work; if your example is not around for them to follow, they will emulate those which are, for good or ill.
- The process of getting to know staff as people as well as job-holders creates a sense of caring, which provides a firm and secure base from which feedback and appraisal will be more readily accepted.
- It creates a more pleasant environment of give and take, where friendly banter and moments of relaxed conversation can relieve tension and reduce the effects of stress.
- It provides the 'lubrication' for managing by walking about and keeping in touch with events and people; problems and opportunities can be picked up at source.
- It reduces the air of secrecy and suspicion which surrounds the unknown and leads to gossip and fantasies about what the boss is really like.

Some of these themes will by now be familiar and I make no apology for repeating the fact that the effectiveness of staff development and people management depends on the quality of relationships between bosses and their subordinates.

The following ways to socialise more at work will be appreciated by your employees as well as setting a good foundation for their development:

- Instead of hiding behind the desk conversing with your favourite cactus, get out and about in the office, the store, the factory floor, the canteen – especially the canteen, or anywhere else where people relax.
- Put people at ease when you meet them, even if you have to open the conversation with last night's episode of EastEnders or Saturday's soccer match.

- Let your hair down now and again. Join in works parties, dances and celebrations – if you don't have them, introduce them.

One very professional head of an elderly people's home dressed up as a Christmas fairy and recited a comic poem by the Christmas tree – an exercise that went down very well with the staff and residents, but in no way diminished her authority or regard. In fact it probably enhanced both by showing the child inside the parent (as discussed in section 5)

- Enter interdepartmental sports or cultural activities, and always buy a few raffle tickets when they circulate the workplace. It demonstrates a generous and caring nature, especially if you never win anything.
- Join your team for coffee or lunch from time to time, or invite them to join you, and regularly hold conversations with them which are not about work, but about you, them, or mutual interests.

If you haven't done this before, or you feel awkward about it, don't go overboard with the idea at first – everyone might think you've started spying on them if you suddenly come out of purdah and start popping up all over the place. Tell your secretary, or your team at the end of a briefing meeting, that you intend to get around the place a bit more and spend less time in your office. You could start by wandering about a bit at break time with a coffee in your hand.

If you are one of life's sociable characters who is never short of a light and friendly word or two with anyone, you may wonder why it should be necessary to write this chapter at all. But there are a surprisingly large number of people who find this difficult, especially at work, and many who think that being the boss means that they have to cut themselves off from people, as if their authority is somehow leached out of them by real contact with subordinates – in fact it is quite the reverse. Someone could get rich returns from starting a charm school for managers!

35

Listen

After attending a very enjoyable communications course some years ago, I sent my tutor a little gift of a wall poster depicting a rather concerned but friendly looking gorilla, with the caption, 'I know you believe you understand what I said, but I'm not sure you realise that what you heard was not what I meant'.

Those of us fortunate enough to be able to hear are not always blessed with the ability to listen! On average, people can think and process incoming information at four times the speed at which they can talk. (Of course there are always the exceptions who seem to talk faster than anyone else can listen!) This fact should give us a great advantage in being able to listen with our full attention, so that we get the underlying 'ideas' message as well as the superficial facts. But most of us spend that time-lag thinking up what we're going to say when the other person stops, and if they don't stop soon enough, rather than forget our gem of wisdom, we interrupt.

The term 'active listening' is used to differentiate from simply absorbing passively what is heard. It demands frequent eye contact, concentrating totally on the person who is talking (i.e. not thinking what you will say next, looking at the clock or looking through the window at a dog crossing the road), sitting in an open relaxed position, and making the sounds and facial expressions of interest from time to time.

It also means listening with our eyes. Researchers vary an their estimates of how much of effective communication is achieved by non-verbal as opposed to verbal behaviour, but the figures are all high – around 45-60 per cent of the impact of our messages comes from body movement rather than the words we speak.

This information comes from gestures, posture, facial expressions, eye movements, and skin tone, all of which are lost during telephone conversations, which could account for why they often create more confusion than they resolve. It also means that the boss who continues signing letters while he says to his subordinate without looking up, 'Carry on, I'm listening', is not, and could be losing out on a lot of information, not just about the facts but about the person.

'Active listening' is a two-way activity. Listeners have to be able to communicate back to talkers that they have understood and check out that they have by briefly paraphrasing and summarising from time to time with such expressions as, 'Yes I understand that it must have been difficult for you to ...', 'If I get you right, what you're suggesting is that we ...', or 'So, what you're saying is ...'

It is a paradox that, as children, the ability to listen is often conditioned out of us by being told, 'Don't interrupt when grown-ups are talking'. Making children keep quiet while others talk does not encourage listening, it associates talking with the power which adults have, while the powerless have to sit silent. In later life, we demonstrate our authority, intelligence and wit by being the ones who talk rather than the ones who listen. We've all heard the tourist abroad who can't understand the local language, try to get what she wants by shouting even louder, or the 'WhenI' bores who begin every sentence, 'When I was ... in the Punjab ... down the Amazon ... talking to Lord ... There are other reasons why we don't listen. We are predisposed to hear what we want to hear - 'You're getting a 30 per cent pay rise' instead of 'You're getting a 13 per cent pay rise.'

There may be certain phrases that always turn us off: 'You ought to ...', 'You always ...', and our minds leap to, 'No, I don't' and we haven't listened to what it is. We may be too interested in the impression we are giving; preoccupied with the wart on the speaker's nose; distracted by interruptions, lack of time, or other pressing business; have something else on our mind; or be just too tired.

Other strong barriers to listening, especially in the workplace, are the listener's perception of the status or credibility of the talker, the fear of having existing opinions challenged, misinterpreting the meaning of the words used, and trying to avoid potential conflict by 'not wanting to know' where people's problems are concerned.

If talking is so pleasant for our egos, and it is so difficult to listen, why go to all the bother?

People who don't listen really don't understand and can't communicate. The worst that could happen is that they're the ones who press that little red button!

But it is more constructive to list the benefits, particularly those which aid staff development or remove barriers to it.

- Listening improves the quality and accuracy of information being transferred, and reduces error.
- It improves the speed and effectiveness of communication throughout an organisation, and outside it, to customers and clients.
- It enables a deeper understanding of an individual, his/her aspirations, needs and potential.
- The attention given during listening acts as a form of recognition and appreciation of the individual who is talking.
- It encourages subordinates to develop themselves by talking through

and solving their own problems, rather than stunting their growth by giving them an answer they did not have to reach for.

- Mutual listening builds up good personal relationships on which all staff development is based.
- Being listened to releases and reduces tensions built up by stress and pressures of work.
- It develops the listener's own faculties for thought and understanding.
- It develops the listener's skills at handling people; you can't effectively manage something you know little about.
- It enables the listener to learn also to listen to themselves and understand better what they 'see' there.

When we don't listen, we run the risk of discouraging subordinates from expressing their ideas, or deflating them by showing off our superior knowledge and building up our egos at the expense of theirs. By contradicting and interrupting we demonstrate to them the low esteem in which they are held.

None of us can be good listeners all the time. On occasions, we cannot resist putting on our 'listening face' to the person speaking to us, while really our ears are tuned into the conversation going on a few feet away. Our need to talk may be greater than our ability to listen – even good listeners need a good listener sometimes. But without trying to be saints, few of us can claim there is no room for improvement.

Resources
Techniques can be followed up in *Listening: the Forgotten Skill*, Madelyn Burley-Allen (John Wiley & Sons, 1982).

36

Counsel

Counselling as a specialist service has been available to employees in many larger organisations for some years. Redundancies resulting from mergers and recessions, as well as career planning, created a need for counselling at work, which has increased since the invention of the 'mid-life crisis' and the discovery of the male menopause. The use of counselling techniques is also becoming part of the normal role of the manager, as it is recognised that people bring into the workplace their whole selves. They cannot be separated off from the effects of attitudes and feelings which arise from past, present and private lives like creaming off curds from milk to make cheese. Domestic situations, good and bad, influence people's performance at work. Anyone with a baby who cries half the night and a 'deaf' spouse will confirm that. On the other hand, an addition to the family of a big new mortgage can spur efforts towards promotion, which sometimes result in overwork and stress.

Work too can impinge very strongly on life outside work for individuals and their families. Difficult shifts, assignments abroad, unrealistic or frequent deadlines, uncertainty and conflict can all affect performance at home.

In either of these situations, it is quite legitimate, and indeed very desirable, that subordinates should seek from their bosses some assistance in working through the problem at a counselling interview. This does not imply that the subordinates are weak, incompetent or sick. It means simply that they have the good sense to realise they are in a difficult situation and need some outside help to come to terms with their feelings, to analyse the problem, identify a range of options, and provide support in their choice of action. If the impact of other circumstances on work performance is marked and looks likely to continue, or a personal crisis arises at work, it is also open to the boss to offer counselling, either by himself or by a specialist, as a means of assistance.

Counselling techniques can also be used pro-actively as a means of staff development or to remove barriers to development, whether these are associated with out-of-work influences or not. Feelings and attitudes about work, about fellow employees, about the boss or about the future, can all create barriers to learning that are more effectively tackled by counselling than other methods. This also applies to developing people for work or promotion, which may be personally very demanding upon them, or require major decisions about life styles and aspirations. Opportunities as well as problems can be a cue for counselling.

Counselling is likely to be the most effective method of managing a situation in which a subordinate is coming to terms with strong feelings, facing up to reality, and deciding on a course of action which may need a lot of commitment to sustain. The counsellor's role is to provide the environment, stimulus and support which enables the subordinate to achieve this him- or herself.

There is no suggestion that managers should replace professional counsellors or that they are equipped to do so. It is important to be able to recognise when the nature of the problem, the person concerned, or the stage your own counselling role has reached, requires the services of a qualified and experienced counsellor. But there are many situations when a manager can use counselling to the lasting benefit of subordinates, their work, the department and indeed themselves. To do so successfully needs training and an attitude of genuine caring.

From the point of view of staff development, as opposed to personal or family crisis, there are numerous indications for using counselling to develop staff in their work or in their own capacity to deal with difficult situations, such as:

- during formal appraisal interviews
- before assignments abroad, in conjunction with training on 'culture shock' and local conditions
- when there are career conflicts and uncertainties, and 'stuck' middle managers
- when there are difficulties between colleagues, between subordinates and the people who report to them, or conflict resulting from 'office politics'
- when someone exhibits symptoms of stress, work overload, or 'workaholism'
- before and during promotions, particularly to posts where the 'new' subordinates were previously the boss's own peer group
- when a subordinate's work is of an emotionally demanding nature, e.g. in the caring professions when dealing with other people's feelings and life or death issues
- after major disappointments, e.g. lost promotion or a real 'danger' at work
- after a major success/victory.

Before considering how to go about counselling, it is important to be clear on how it differs from other regular interactions between a boss and his or her subordinates. There are basically three different approaches to helping people in their work, or anywhere else for that matter.

First, we can tell them what to do. This concentrates solely on the task not the person, and creates dependence on us, the teller. But there are obviously situations when this is the best method, e.g. in a case of extreme urgency or when technical/factual data is all that is required at the time.

Second, we can coach them. In this method we are dealing with a combination of the person and the task, encouraging subordinates to think and analyse for themselves by means of a questioning approach, with inputs of information when required, and leaving them to make their own decisions, with feedback afterwards on the results.

Third, we can counsel them. This focuses entirely upon the individual. The counsellor's role is to enable and encourage them to see their own situation and its implications more clearly, possibly suggest alternative solutions, but leave the subordinate to reach his or her own decision, without making suggestions concerning the solution, and without giving feedback on it or even knowing in detail what it is.

The differences in focus, and in the role of 'helper' are vital to successful counselling. The situation can be damaging without them.

There are certain difficulties inherent in the work context which you will need to overcome in order to be able to counsel.

- **Time.** It is a time-consuming activity and a session is unlikely to take less than half an hour to an hour, which should be totally without interruption of any kind.

- **Your position of authority.** Obviously if a subordinate does not want to discuss the matter with you (after all, you may be the problem!), you will obviously offer counselling from someone else, within or outside the organisation, and without any recrimination. If you have a good relationship with staff this is unlikely to be a problem, but the fact that you are an authority figure will be, unless you set an environment that enables you both to meet in an atmosphere of equality and trust.

- **Your motive.** There must be a genuine desire on your part to want the individual to develop through counselling. There will probably be benefits in performance as a result, but the subordinate must not feel manipulated to comply with company goals or your own needs. Your motive has to be the truly unselfish wish to enable the subordinate to develop him- or herself.

The following is a brief guide to the steps in carrying out a counselling interview.

First, allow sufficient time and ensure there are no interruptions from any source. Pick a venue that is informal, quiet and comfortable. A good arrangement is two comfortable chairs either side of a low table but not exactly opposite each other. Take 10 minutes beforehand to review your knowledge of the person. (To open the interview with enquiries about the family when in fact he or she is not even married is not a good start.) Consciously detach your image of the person from common stereotypes – emotional women, dyed-in-the-wool engineers, cocky graduates. You will be dealing with a unique person not a label.

Second, do not take notes throughout the interview, as it will create a barrier to communication and destroy the atmosphere of trust and frankness. Your opening remarks will depend on which of you has initiated the session, but they should be warm and general, to allow time to 'tune-in' to each other. If you suggested the session, e.g. because someone appears to be over-stressed at work, you will already have said what it is you would like to have a quiet talk about.

Thereafter the interview roughly follows four stages, which should be allowed to flow naturally from one to the other, or with gentle guidance if one stage seems to be sticking without making any progress.

1. Identifying the problem

Ask them to tell you about the problem. Let them take their time. If necessary, help with simple questions. Listen carefully, i.e. employ 'active listening', which means maintaining regular but not piercing eye contact, being aware of non-verbal communication, and not thinking about what you are going to say next. Frequently, the problem first described is the one which they are able to recognise more readily, but there may be an underlying problem they have either not realised or they have been avoiding.

Encourage them to look more deeply at the situation, with such questions as 'What else do you think might be causing this?', 'Why is it a problem to you?' or 'What have you tried doing so far?' Working out why earlier actions have not resolved a problem will sometimes reveal deeper causes.

Never at any stage in the interview criticise anything the other person says or has done by saying, e.g. 'You shouldn't get upset about it' or 'That was a silly thing to do'. It will halt further progress in the interview. Your intention is to help your subordinate get to the root of his/her problem; to make judgements about what is revealed in the process is an abuse of trust amounting to psychological violence.

It is helpful throughout the interview to paraphrase what has been said occasionally. This reflects back to subordinates the picture they are putting together, and it can help you guide them to the next stage if you think they are ready. Once the core problem has been identified, encourage them to examine their feelings about it. They may have begun this process quite naturally already.

2. Accepting feelings

Help the individual to recognise and accept the feelings being experienced as a result of the problem with such questions as 'What did you feel like when ...?' or 'How do you feel now about ...?' All the questions you ask during a counselling session should aim to help the other person see the situation more clearly, or guide him or her to look in other directions if you think that would help, and not to give you a fuller picture or to satisfy a natural curiosity about events.

Try to put yourself in the other person's place. As one eminent counsellor once said, it is trying to put yourself into the other person's shoes without wanting to stay there.

If you have had a similar experience to the one being presented, it will be easier for you to do this, but in most cases it is better to do no more than allude to the fact. There is a temptation to offer your own solution as theirs, or they may think you are doing so. The focus should remain on the person being counselled, with a minimum of input from you – everyone's reactions to problems are unique anyway.

3. Exploring alternatives

Using the same kind of open questioning and listening techniques, encourage the individual to identify alternative responses to the problem, and the realistic implications of each. Useful phrases are 'Have you considered ...?' and 'What do you think would happen if ...?' But don't rush into suggestions until people have had time to explore as many as they can for themselves. They should determine the direction they want to follow. At this point you are enabling them to draw upon inner strengths they may not have been aware of. Too much direction from you may prevent that development.

4. Making the decision

This has to be done entirely by the person you are counselling, because he or she has to be fully committed to it. You can help with such questions as 'When do you have to make a decision?' 'What do you think you will do now?' or 'When/where/how do you think you might do that?'

Of course they may decide not to take any action. They may wish to go away and give more consideration to options, or get further information. No advice should be given, or pressure as to how they should decide to act. Don't use such expressions as 'What you ought to do is ...' or 'You should really ...'

It is not easy to let people come to what you may feel is the wrong decision, but it is they who have to live with the outcome and it does not help to give 'secondhand' solutions or take away their confidence in the decision they have just made.

There should be enough time to wind down the interview without an abrupt stop which leaves you both 'in the air'. The person you are counselling should feel the satisfaction of having fully explored the problem, and knowing what personal follow-up they want to do.

It will be apparent that counselling is not easy. Training and practice make it more so, as does the general climate created by your management style. Regular close contact with subordinates facilitates the use of a counselling role. It also makes it easier to recognise when it might be called for. The ability to use this approach acceptably with your staff is a good base from which to manage generally. It enables people to learn a strategy for coping with future problems and opportunities, and so aids personal development.

Counselling need not be confined to the boss/subordinate relationship, for colleagues can counsel each other and often do. Counselling at work, as anywhere else, is legitimate and valuable, but it is important to recognise when professional counselling should be offered.

Resources

Counselling People at Work: An Introduction for Managers, Robert de Board (Gower, 1983) goes into more detail about the techniques and their application, including a useful section on the use of counselling during appraisal interviews. Although now out of print, a good library should be able to find you a copy of this good book.

37

Appraise for Development

I was tempted to begin this chapter with the suggestion that if your organisation's appraisal scheme consists of a densely laid out form in triplicate (copies to personnel, central records and the head of department), and covers every conceivable purpose from pay and promotion to training and performance, file it in the wastepaper basket and start again, because the best appraisal form for developing staff is a blank sheet of paper. But I won't, because this book aims to be practical and the reality of the situation is probably that you are already stuck with the prevailing appraisal policy and the personnel officer's pet system and have to make the best of it. Whatever formal appraisal scheme you have to operate, the way you handle it can help to overcome the system's shortcomings, and be a development opportunity for your subordinate.

Good bosses are informally appraising their staff all the time through regular feedback, but this is appraisal 'on the hoof', given briefly, frequently and related to current tasks and targets. No formal annual appraisal is likely to be effective unless this feedback is given in between times, but there are some development advantages to a major annual assessment for the appraiser and the 'appraisee':

- It gives a longer perspective into the past and the future for reviewing experience, direction and career planning.
- It enables a detailed appraisal not only of the individual's performance but of the job itself and the targets which have been set.
- It provides a significant amount of uninterrupted time to concentrate exclusively on the employee, and should help to develop closer understanding between you.
- You both have the opportunity beforehand to reflect on the past and raise issues for which there is rarely an appropriate moment at other time, e.g. to dispel underlying 'niggles'.
- It enables employees to feedback to you, in an atmosphere of privileged exchange of views, other factors which affect their performance and that of the department. One of them might be their boss! It is a chance

for you both to be honest within the protection that this confidential 'ritual' gives you.

But the appraisal interview will be more effective and much easier to handle if people work in an environment where regular feedback is expected and understood. If annual appraisal is the only time a manager talks to his or her staff about how they are doing, they have a problem which no amount of interview skills training will solve.

Take a positive attitude towards the appraisal interview. It should be an opportunity for you both, not a trial by ordeal. If the appraisal form you have to use is the proverbial obstacle race, or even if it isn't, ignore it for the time being. Don't start the interview with your pen poised over a row of multiple choice questions, squinting across the desk at your hapless subordinate while you decide which box to tick.

A couple of weeks beforehand, let subordinates know when and where the interview will be. Outline the purpose and format and ask them to spend some time reviewing their own performance in relation to agreed targets and objectives: things that went well, things that haven't gone well, the direction they feel they should take at work and in their career, and their particular strengths and weaknesses. Suggest it might help if they wrote down a few notes for their own use, including any issues they would like to raise with you. Tell them that you will be doing the same. You can even give them a copy of the official form ,if one exists, so that they can see where you are coming from.

The environment of the interview is important for the confidence and comfort of you both. Budget sufficient time, an hour and a half at the very least. Ensure there are no interruptions, not even for coffee – have this brought in first if you wish but don't begin the serious business of the interview while you are both still trying to drink it.

The seating arrangements will depend on the nature of your relationship. One chief executive in the public sector does not have a desk in his office at all on principle. His subordinates are used to sitting across from a comfortable chair for face-to-face discussion. If this is not your practice, the unaccustomed proximity and informality may in fact unnerve people. Some people find 'spaces between' difficult to cope with. But don't go to the other extreme and have him or her perched on a small hard chair while you gaze imperiously at the hapless individual from behind six feet of polished mahogany status symbol.

A pretty safe bet is to be seated on comfortable chairs either side of a low table, but not exactly opposite each other, which may be seen as a confrontation position.

To prepare for the interview, make a few notes on the items you want to cover. This enables you to concentrate thoroughly on the discussion without trying to remember them at the same time. Clarify to yourself what aspects of the subordinate's performance you want to develop as a result of the appraisal.

Don't let the fact that appraisal is part of a formal system, and has associated documentation, turn you into a pontificating headmaster. Use a questioning technique, with open questions, which encourage thoughtful and analytical responses rather than one word answers, and avoid leading questions. Choose 'Tell me about some of the successes/problems you've had this year' rather than 'You had quite a success/problem with the new marketing plan, didn't you?' The other person should be doing the talking 80 per cent of the time and you should be listening for 100 per cent of the time, i.e. 'listening' to non-verbal behaviour even when you are talking.

Encourage your subordinates to discuss their strengths and weaknesses and adopt a joint problem-solving approach to build on the former and either improve upon, or reduce the impact of, the latter. Make it clear that you are helping them to appraise their work, not judging them as people. The session should include the opportunity for them to talk about reasons for shortfalls other than their own performance. Interdependencies exist in most jobs and it is only fair to consider their influence for good or bad upon the performance being appraised.

Maintain the feedback approach of mixing praise with constructive suggestions for improvement. (Destructive criticism is counter-productive and has no place in appraisal.) Negative feedback must be based on agreed standards and measurement of performance, and before embarking on it, check that they are aware of what these standards are and understand how they are measured. There was a case where the first time a subordinate became aware of the standards expected of her was when she was told at the appraisal interview that she had not met them. This is an extremely uncomfortable and potentially disastrous position for both parties.

Where regular feedback is part of your management style, the method will already be familiar and acceptable to your subordinates, and more likely therefore to produce the results you want. It will also enable you to refer to previous feedback and to reinforce it if necessary. A cautionary word on criticism. It is better not used, but if you do criticise, never make comparisons with other people, and never criticise what you have assumed to be your subordinate's motives and attitudes. It may be an underlying problem but you will never be able to tackle it unless you get him or her to tell you about it.

To increase the learning potential of an appraisal interview, the pattern of the session should follow the stages of the learning cycle (described more fully in Chapter 4):

1. **Experience** – factual discussions of tasks undertaken and how they were done.
2. **Reflection** – review of performance from different aspects, considering alternatives.
3. **Conceptualisation** – drawing conclusions, separating causes from symptoms, working out new targets and intentions for further development.

4. **Experimentation** – planning and implementing the agreed action with feedback/training and adjustments as necessary. From this follows the next period of experience.

We are all better at some of these stages than others. If the person being appraised is less confident at conceptualising, for example, you may have to be more directive in suggesting courses of action, but allow time for his or her own ideas too. On the other hand, some subordinates may be stronger on reflection than you are. If so, let them take the lead while you listen and evaluate.

It is useful to summarise at intervals during the discussion to keep you both clear on where you've got to and to check out the other person's understanding and agreement. Keep a few notes on the interview, both the process and the action agreed, and let your subordinate have a copy.

Everything that is written down during an appraisal interview should be shown to the person appraised. If it is good news, why leave them in uncertainty, feeling they are not appreciated? If it is bad news, hiding the truth will not enable them to develop and improve. The finally completed appraisal form too should be seen and agreed by the subordinate. Secrecy breeds suspicion and anxiety, which are not conducive to development and can be damaging to the person. If there are areas on which agreement cannot be reached, then subordinates' dissent should be noted on the form with their reasons.

The form should be completed while you are both together (if a lot of factual background information is required, this can be filled in before the interview to save time). This stage of the interview is a good time to complete it and discuss it.

Up until this point, the focus of the interview will have been on both the tasks and the individuals' performance in carrying them out. Once the appraisal has been written down and shared, the focus of attention should be on the individuals for the remainder of the interview. The purpose of this is to help them to accept the agreed appraisal, look at the implications for themselves and draw their own conclusions as to what they should do about it. Your approach should be that of counselling and open questioning: 'How do you feel about the conclusions we have reached?' 'What do you see as your alternatives?' 'Have you thought about ...?', 'What do you think would happen if ...?' Your main concern at this part of the interview is the person's reaction and attitude to what has taken place during the appraisal, not the work output.

A final summing up is essential so that you both know what is to take place in the immediate future, and neither of you leaves the interview feeling there are 'loose ends' lying as unfinished business to create concern. Conclude the interview with positive encouragement. Even if he or she is an unmitigated disaster, find a constructive note on which to end – if only to wish them well in their future elsewhere!

As you close the door on your subordinate, you may heave a sigh of relief and reach for the hospitality cupboard. But the appraisal interview is not the end. It is the beginning of a new working cycle, and if you have done it well, a new period of learning and motivation as well. Much will depend on the monitoring and feedback which follows the formal appraisal, and any course of action promised by you, such as further training or other development activities, must be carried out.

After your experience, reflect on how it went and what you might have done differently, and experiment with improved techniques for the next time. If the documentation really is awful, make this a priority for trying to get it improved.

Resources

There is a lot of material about the design and implementation of appraisal systems, but for the practical application by managers try *Managing the Poor Performer*, V. Stewart and A. Stewart (Gower, 1988). See also the chapter on counselling during appraisal in *Counselling People at Work:An Introduction for Managers*, by Robert de Board.

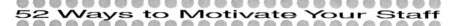
38

Inform and Involve

'Feed 'em on muck and keep 'em in the dark' may be sound advice for growing mushrooms. But when applied to employees, as it has been on some notable occasions in the past, it can lead to long, bitter disputes in which no one is the winner.

Senior management's responsibility to communicate with employees at operational and management level, and to provide opportunities for participation, has become more widely recognised in recent years, sometimes as a result of hard lessons. Without accurate, clear and timely information from the company itself, the grapevine can be a vicious weed, stretching its tendrils of misunderstanding and uncertainty to every corner of the organisation, strangling goodwill and common sense.

This is not helped by the media and the trades unions themselves communicating effectively with your employees – they each have their own job to do and their own interpretation of what they see as the facts, which may be no more than the rotted fruit of the same vine. In a time of change, especially, situations can become volatile very quickly, and change nowadays seems to be an almost continuous process.

But it is not only to avoid confrontation that employee communication and participation are important, they are essential ingredients in the development and commitment of staff. If you want to encourage your people to increase their skills, performance and commitment, and apply them to their jobs, they need to know:

- What you and they are really there for, what the organisation stands for, and what its major policies are.

- How their goals and targets relate to those of the unit, division, company and corporation as a whole.

- How well they are achieving their goals, how this relates to other's achievements and contributes to the organisation's performance.

161

- How the company is doing nationally and internationally, and its relationship to the rest of the market and the economy.

- What changes are taking place, or are imminent, which affect them directly and less directly.

- General news both good and bad about company events and the people in it, so that they can feel part of the culture and value system of a living entity.

However it is they are told, they need the opportunity to communicate back. A lot of organisations have a system for cascading information down from the boardroom and the executive suite, but they don't wait for a reply. Bottom-up communication is just as important for the following reasons:

☑ It provides a means of checking out that the message has been accurately received and understood.

☑ It enables staff to contribute ideas and points of view as a form of participation; they feel more commitment to what they are asked to do, and you may get some sound ideas in return, especially if they have a genuine stake in success.

☑ Two-way communication gives employees a greater understanding of the role of management, and the constraints and opportunities within which decision-making at a senior level has to take place.

☑ It enables management to receive feedback on the quality of the communication process, and the message itself.

☑ Employees know what information they need to have and the means they find most effective. Unless a company is prepared to accept that its employees have a right, within reason, to determine the information they are given and how they are given it, then it should question its own motives in having a communication policy. If it is genuinely non-manipulative, there should be no problem other than industrial security, and this is rarely a major problem in practice.

The Japanese are better than almost any other nation at direct, close communication which is genuinely two-way and has no barriers of status to get in the way of understanding. They even have an expression for it -'talking knee to knee'.

Verbal, small-group communication is the most effective (although facts, figures and illustrations can be distributed in written form for ease of reference), because it allows for discussion and explanation. It also demonstrates more personal commitment to the message on behalf of the message-bearer – you don't get the non-verbals in an annual report or a monthly bulletin, especially the tongue-in-cheek or the fingers-crossed-behind-the-back bits!

Some chief executives and managing directors address the entire assembled company or a division at a time on particularly important occasions or as part of an annual company conference. Useful though this may be, there is little chance for two-way communication, other than heckling, and once a year is hardly enough to keep people adequately informed.

Information and involvement should be direct, relevant, frequent, clear and accurate, and should include everyone – not excluding the receptionist sitting among the potted plants in the foyer. Timing is also important. If you are too slow, the grapevine or the media will have got in first and may condition the acceptance of your own message; if you are too quick, the information may still be uncertain and have to be corrected later – not a good way to gain credibility.

It may seem unnecessarily obvious to say that employee communications should be designed to be in a language and format to optimise understanding. If it is not, and is done simply to fulfil the letter of company policy rather than the spirit of genuine communication, it will be counter-productive to say the least.

Briefing groups

The concept of briefing groups, pioneered by the Industrial Society, fulfils the requirements of effective information and involvement if carried out in a sincere desire to communicate. It also achieves this in a way that gives particular scope for staff development.

Groups of employees (up to a maximum of 20 to allow for discussion) meet at least once a month for half an hour (depending on the number and complexity of items), to be briefed by their immediate boss, who has already been briefed by his or her boss and so on all the way up and down the line until everyone is included. It needs planning, co-ordination and supervision to ensure that the content of the original briefing at director level reaches the shop-floor through each successive level as quickly as possible. The length and frequency of briefings will depend on the situation; during a period of major change, shorter but more frequent briefings may be necessary both to keep up with events and to ensure that the response is fed rapidly backup the line again. (Sources of further information on setting up briefing groups are given at the end of the chapter).

For the system to be credible and effective, there has to be commitment from management at the very top, and from senior and middle managers to ensure that briefings are taking place as planned. But even with commitment all round, how well it works will depend to a large extent on the communication abilities of each supervisor and manager.

An important part of the supervision of the system is not just the existence of briefings but the identification and implementation of training needs in communication and presentation skills. In this respect, it can have valuable development spin-off, transferable to other areas of supervision and management. There is a range of other media commonly used for employee communications. House journals, annual reports, handbooks, videos and the intranet can all be useful and informative, and can have development spin-off for the staff producing them, but they are essentially one-way, impersonal and not immediate enough or sufficiently flexible to deal with real 'news' as opposed to information. Weekly news bulletins and individual letters in pay packets are more topical, as are notice boards (but I have yet to meet anyone who admits to reading the latter).

> A petro-chemical firm, with a fairly small workforce of highly skilled operators (about 300), operates an 'open meetings' policy. With very few exceptions, any management or departmental meeting can be attended by employees after first checking out their absence with their supervisor. Apart from the good relations resulting from the fact that this is possible, and the amount of mutual trust shown thereby, the information they get is straight from the horses' mouths.

All these media, together with company conferences, departmental meetings and working lunches, can be used for background information or as back-up to a more regular small-group two-way communication system. The flow of information from the bottom up can also be enhanced as an exercise in its own right through employee surveys, regular management contact in operational zones, and 'employee ideas' schemes.

There is only one thing worse for employee relations than having no communications policy, and that is having a policy that doesn't work. If your organisation does have a formal system, it is worth considering the following questions:

- How good is the quantity and quality of information being passed down to you or made available to you?

- What opportunities do you have to question, ask for reasons, clarification or more information?

- How effective are the means of communication in delivering the message, e.g. in timing, clarity, relevance, frequency, accuracy? Are they two-way and face-to-face?

- How good are you at communicating downwards, and how good are your subordinates, in their turn?

- How effective are the means for communication being passed back up the line, and who listens?

- How well is the system maintained, monitored and evaluated?

If your organisation does not have a communications policy, start asking questions. Not only can few organisations afford not to have one, but the absence of an effective system to inform and involve employees is a major constraint upon the management of your department and the development of your staff. It may be leaving you out in the cold too.

39

Respect Your Team

The word 'respect' has accumulated biblical connotations of deferring to others, who, for various reasons, are deemed to know better – like our elders. This is unfortunate because what it really means is to give heed and consideration to others' rights to be who they are, and to value what they value. Children have as much right to respect as elders, and subordinates have as much right to respect as bosses.

Respect is the basis of good relations. It is therefore essential to staff development and to self-development. Without it, people just do not develop, whatever sophisticated techniques or facilities may be engaged to train them. It does not mean you have to agree with them, or even like them particularly. Many a boss is not exactly top of the popularity poll, and yet is highly respected at both ends of the hierarchy – frequently because of the respect she or he demonstrates towards others, especially staff.

The other important thing about respect is that if you don't give it, you certainly don't get it. It doesn't just mean that men take their hats off when they come into the office, or refrain from telling blue jokes in front of their secretaries. Respect, or lack of it, is demonstrated in all manner of verbal and non-verbal signals we give all the time, sometimes unconsciously. These give us away every day, by revealing our true attitudes towards people.

To begin thinking about respect, particularly for those over whom we have recognised, structural authority, we have to reflect on our own feelings and all the little things we do to reveal them. We may show lack of trust by not delegating power as well as work or by hoarding information others could benefit from. By telling people rather than asking them to do things, which demands their compliance rather than our expecting and respecting their willing agreement, we say, 'You are lazy and unmotivated so I'm telling you, and then you'll have to do it because I'm your boss'. Asking people does not deny their motivation, it acknowledges it and gives it direction and purpose.

A boss who interprets a subordinate's assertiveness as disrespectful reveals more about his or her own lack of confidence than the subordinate's assumed lack of respect. A good sign of mutual respect is the ability for both parties to be assertive in staring their position or their needs, in such a way that compromise or collaboration resolves the differences, or else lack of agreement can be recognised and accepted, depending on the situation.

Another common symptom of the lack of respect is to criticise rather than to give constructive feedback (especially if the criticism is given behind someone's back). How often have you heard someone describe an errant subordinate as a 'cretin', or a boss whose decision isn't agree with as an 'idiot'? Casual comments like this soon cause subordinates to lose respect for both the critic and the boss. We sometimes learn this way of handling authority from school – hearing countless schoolmasters rasp the rhetorical question 'Well, Simpkins, you're not much good are you, boy?' or the positive conditioning approach, 'You're an idiot, Hyde-Smyth – what are you?'

Disrespect for others is not always intentional. It is often the result of conditioning, attitudes absorbed without even realising it, or just not putting ourselves in the other person's shoes to think how they might feel about what we say and do.

To ensure that your well-planned staff development ideas bear fruit, think about some of the regular happenings in your place of work, and reflect on whether you manage with respect:

- When someone makes a mistake, do you respect them for all the times they have been right and help them learn from it for next time; or do you belittle them with criticism as a punishment?

- When you want to see your staff, do you respect their time by agreeing when it is convenient whenever possible; or do you interrupt whatever they are doing whenever it suits you – including your secretary?

- When someone disagrees with your opinion, do you respect their right to hold it and be heard, but explain why you don't intend to act upon it; or do you pull rank and insist they see things from your point of view, and if they don't, keep quiet about it?

- If you are a male and have female subordinates, do you respect them as people doing a job of work regardless of their gender; or do you have fun at their expense with suggestive jokes or demeaning little endearments, which you wouldn't use to male subordinates – not even behind their backs?

- If you are a woman and have male subordinates, do you accept them as individuals doing a job of work; or do you stereotype them as male chauvinists and take your resentment out on them?

- When you want to make changes, improve performance, or influence subordinates' behaviour, do you respect their ability to make reasoned decisions about their actions and accept the implications, by discussing things openly in an atmosphere of mutual trust, or do you manipulate them from hidden agendas and motives you would rather not declare?

- When you give feedback and appraisal, do you respect your subordinates' ability to recognise their own failures and improve upon them with constructive guidance; or do you recount their mistakes and warn them about trouble if they make them again?

- Do you maintain regular informed contact with employee and union representatives to develop a permanent working relationship of mutual respect; or do you ignore them until there is a confrontation and view them only as a negative aspect of your management role?

- Do you accept the prevailing conditions of service and other company policies relating to your staff even if they are unfair and unnecessarily restrictive; or do you go all out to have changes made to improve their working conditions and environment?

It is worth reflecting and increasing our awareness, because not meaning disrespect is not enough. We have to take positive steps to feel respect and to show it, if we want our real intentions to be implemented and accepted. Gamesmanship may be fine sport for the ego, but it has no place in your management style if you want to develop your staff and have a good team.

40

Encourage Assertiveness

Assertiveness is not about manipulation, bossy women, pushy Americans, or salesmen with the gift of the gab to sell their own grandmothers. It is about influencing the behaviour of others in such a way that we stand up for our rights while recognising theirs. What we say and the way we say it preserve the self-esteem of both parties, and are therefore likely to be more effective than being either aggressive or passive.

Assertiveness is based on honesty in expressing our feelings and point of view, combined with caring about the other person and our future relationship with them.

Developing staff depends on a mutually assertive relationship, because honesty and the preservation of self-esteem encourages learning, while aggression tends to create defensiveness or counter-aggression – and may damage the relationship in the future. Passive behaviour is unlikely to effect any change and will eventually erode the authority of the boss, whereas assertiveness encourages mutual respect and can therefore increase our authority.

Obviously, some situations at work dictate the most appropriate form of response. If you've just had a bomb alert, or found someone drunk in charge of a fork-lift truck, you're not too concerned with the niceties of communication theory – in either event there may not be any future relationship to worry about anyway!

But when it is important to you, to the company, or for the development of the individual, that you effectively influence their behaviour without damaging the relationship, then assertiveness is an essential skill to master. For example, it can enable you to say 'no' (to your boss as well as you subordinates), it allows you to correct mistakes in a way that will be acceptable (and therefore effective), and it enables you to change others' behaviour in a non-manipulative way.

Aggression and assertiveness are often confused in discussion, and it may be revealing to look at the way four different bosses handle people when they want to correct them, or change what they do. Their styles could be described as overtly aggressive, covertly aggressive, passive and assertive.

Derek

Derek is overtly aggressive as a manager. He has no difficulty in being honest, in fact he is very outspoken, but at the expense of other people's feelings. He likes to win and be seen as the victor, especially by the one he has had a disagreement with. He 'tells 'em straight', and if he gets any of what he calls 'back chat', says 'You know I'm right, why don't you just admit it?' Derek likes to dominate, and, if thwarted, can be sarcastic and unpleasant, with a lot of glaring and finger-pointing when he talks to you. When things go wrong, he tends to blame others. Because he is confronting in his style, he has to win or else he has a lot of face to lose; consequently, most people who come up against him, especially his subordinates, usually get their self-esteem ground into the floor just to make sure.

When his junior came back from central stores with the wrong piece of equipment, the conversation went something like this. 'You never get it right first time, do you? This is no damn good – why did you let them palm you off with it!' 'Well, they said it would do just as well.' 'And you believed that rubbish, I suppose. Go back and get what I told you to get.' (Withdrawal of junior party, not only feeling an idiot to his boss, but believing the stores think him a dupe too, and not having learned why it is the substitute equipment won't work, nor how to deal more effectively with the stores foreman next time.)

Of course Derek doesn't go on like this all the time; he softens it a bit with his boss, and for all I know he is entirely different away from work. He does have his strengths. He is single-minded in achieving his goals and everyone knows where they are with him (under heel most of the time), but he has a higher staff turnover than his colleagues and is forever having the personnel officer in the place sorting out disciplinary and grievance problems.

Betty

On the other hand, Betty manages in a covertly aggressive style. She has no more consideration for people's rights and feelings than Derek and likes to win just as often, but she doesn't come out with it. Her form of winning is to manipulate circumstances so that she gets the better of people, 'and they never know what hit 'em'. Her staff are unsure how well or poorly they perform because she is not open with them in discussing it, or how they might improve. They might guess by the fact that they have increasingly been left with all the routine or rotten jobs to do, or never get the chance to deal with the more important clients. There is no confrontation or visible conflict in her department, personnel staff are rarely called in to sort out people problems, but there is a lot of suspicion and back-watching, and her staff don't work to their full potential.

When Betty was very dissatisfied with the performance of one of her subordinates (actually, she thought – quite wrongly as it happened – that he was being disloyal to the department in the amount of liaison he was doing with another unit), she got her way by withholding information he needed for his work, and undermining his position by sending others to meetings he ought to have attended. The strangulation process was slow but effective – he eventually resigned.

Bernard

Bernard's style of managing is passive. He is very concerned about the needs and feelings of his subordinates, so much so that he avoids any conflict or unpleasantness and takes the rap himself for the poor returns his department puts in. It's not that he is over-keen to be popular; in fact he is rather inhibited socially. This lack of communication leads to uncertainties among his staff as to their goals and achievements, and they sometimes go off in different directions, or seek decisions from his deputy. Bernard works extremely hard – if anyone wants to go on a course or have extra time off, he invariably says 'yes', and then tries to make up the work by doing himself work he ought to delegate.

When he tackled someone recently about bad time-keeping, he was hesitant and apologetic. The subordinate took advantage of this and the conversation ended up with Bernard saying 'Well, try to come in on time and if you can't, at least don't let the boss see you'.

Bernard does feel frustrated and angry sometimes, especially when he knows people are taking advantage of him, but it tends to be turned in on himself. He did go off the deep end once. It was over some silly little thing which his secretary always did, but he had never told her how much it irritated him, until one day, when his frustration over other things had built up to such an extent that this was just the last straw. To hear him you'd have thought it was Derek on a really bad day. The poor woman was so shaken she picked up her handbag and never came back.

Dorothy

Dorothy's natural style is to manage assertively. Not all the time. There are occasions at work when there is too much of a rush to be considerate and she wants it done now, and without any discussion. There are also situations when, although someone's behaviour is not what she would like, it is not affecting her or the department's work to the extent that it is worth making an issue of at the time, and she will ignore it. Her staff understand this flexibility because she is usually consistent and is assertive enough in her day-to-day dealings with them that their self-esteem and sense of achievement are not dented by her manner on occasions when everyone is working at full tilt.

If she wants to change someone's behaviour or improve their performance she will say so openly, and be honest about the way she feels early on, before she gets annoyed about it or it becomes too much of a problem. In fact she usually starts by stating her feelings first, shows that she understands the other person's point of view, keeps to the facts, and gives them a good reason why they should do whatever it is. She listens to them, but unless they have an even better reason why not (and that's rare), she just sticks to her guns until mutual agreement is reached.

When she noticed one of her subordinates had been attending far more conferences and exhibitions than anyone else in the team, and it was beginning to show in the amount of work others had to do to make up for it, she invited him into her office during a quiet time. This is the gist of their discussion:

Dorothy:	John, I am concerned about the number of conferences you have attended lately. I know it is important to you to keep up to date and you do report back on them, but it means that the rest of the team have had to cover for your work rather frequently and I feel this is unfair to them.
John:	I haven't been to all that many.
Dorothy:	From your expense claims it seems to be five in the last two months, and no one else has been to more than one, some to none at all. John: I work as hard as anyone here. And anyway you've never said there was any rule about how many conferences we can attend.
Dorothy:	I agree, you do work hard. I'm not questioning your work, but the number of days you are away from the office on conferences. There has been no hard and fast rule about this, but I think five in two months is unfair on the rest of the team.
John:	Charles Bennet in R and D goes to more than that.
Dorothy:	I am not responsible for what Charles Bennet does, but I am concerned to ensure the fair distribution of workload and conference opportunities in this department.
John:	Well, what do you think is fair then, how many can I go to?
Dorothy:	I think everyone in the team should get the same chance to attend outside events. As you seem to have a good source of information on what's on, I'd like you to make sure everyone else shares it too, and we'll work on a target of four conferences a year for each member of the team, but I think you'd better let everyone else have a go before you attend any more, don't you?
John:	All right, I'll put brochures up on the notice board as I get them. I suppose we could try working out some kind of a rota.

Dorothy: That seems a good idea. Do that, and we'll review the situation in 3 months. Thank you.

Bernard would probably not have broached the subject at all until he had a near riot on his hands from other members of the team. Derek would no doubt have reduced John's 'away days' soon enough, but probably not without some harsh words on his part, and resentment on John's, who would have learned not to attend so many conferences to keep the boss quiet but not the need to develop a greater sense of responsibility towards his fellow team members in sharing information and opportunities. And I dread to think what Betty would have done to him!

Most people do not like imposed solutions, even if they realise they've been in the wrong. Compliance may be only short-term, whereas commitment to a shared solution represents positive development and can deepen relationships.

If handling the situation assertively does not work, you always have the option if necessary of insisting upon what you want done or not done. If you start with aggression, you set a pattern from which you cannot withdraw subsequently without losing face.

Assertiveness will not usually work unless both parties basically care about the relationship. Some situations simply can't be rescued, either because the relationship has become so bad that there is no mutual respect left, or one or other side just doesn't care, or is recognised as being insincere in the sentiments being expressed. Insincerity or bad faith turns assertiveness into manipulation and rarely fools anyone.

The benefits to you, the boss, of being able to use assertive behaviour when you want to are fairly obvious:

- It enables you to change unwanted behaviour without damaging relationships (it often strengthens them).
- It enables you to give negative feedback without diminishing people's self-esteem, and without either of you losing face.
- Your staff (and superiors) have a greater commitment to agreed changes or action.
- Your staff learn and develop from the experience.
- You can say 'no' without creating resentment, e.g. to promotion requests or to your boss's attempt to offload too much on to you.
- Problems are dealt with before feelings ride too high or the effects get out of hand.
- It keeps your blood pressure down!

There are additional benefits in encouraging employees to be more assertive in their dealings with each other, with others in the organisation, and with customers and suppliers:

- It manages conflict before it becomes destructive.

- It creates better external relations for the company.
- It increases the effectiveness of inter-departmental relationships, which saves both time and needless 'aggro' with financial control or stores, etc.
- The team pulls together better with the increased openness and the mutual respect which results.
- It creates a team of winners, with high self-esteem, both of which are essential for continued development and personal growth.
- It encourages self-correction, as people learn to take more responsibility for the effects of their own behaviour upon others and the work of the department.

But the real test of your own self-esteem and ability to be assertive (i.e. both candid and caring), is for you to recognise the benefits in your subordinates being assertive to you – and to encourage it! Consider the following:

- Assertive behaviour is most effective in producing mutually beneficial changes when both parties practise it simultaneously.
- It develops thinking, caring and responsibility in subordinates towards their bosses.
- It develops self-esteem and self-confidence.
- It enables your staff to let you know of things you do which adversely affect their work – to your face, e.g. saying 'no' when you delegate more than they can effectively cope with, allocating work, etc., which bypasses the supervisor and undermines his/her authority, interrupting people unnecessarily and disrupting their attempts at time-management, demanding work be typed immediately and then not signing it for 2 days.
- It increases their respect for you, and therefore your authority.
- It helps to create a learning environment and a more pleasant place in which to work.

Everyone has the right to make his or her needs and opinions known and to negotiate a solution. It is not so much what we say that is important, but the way we say it. If you want somewhere to practise first, try getting better standards in the canteen without upsetting Gladys. Or, if you want less of a challenge to start with, try your local garage next time the car comes back from its service with more faults than it went in with.

Resources

There is a very practical and readable book, *Assertiveness*, by Beels, Hopson and Scally which includes a lot of advice on changing one's own behaviour to deal with a variety of work-related situations. Management Books 2000.

41

Learn from Your Subordinates

No one can know it all. Trying to has been the downfall of many a 'burned-out' manager. The majority of managers, whether in industry or the public services, have moved into their positions from the practice of a specific skill or profession. They may have spent many years perfecting and applying their knowledge, and it often comes hard to let go of some of this expertise in order to concentrate on the new role of managing. Too often, this happens with no appropriate training at all.

But there are compensations. One of the most exciting challenges of management is developing and working through the expertise of others, in order to achieve your vision of success. It is all the more rewarding when that vision is shared by those around you.

However specialised the field, and however professionally competent the manager, to be an effective leader, he or she must add a new dimension to the role, a different orientation. It is like the captain of a submarine who has to spend time looking through the periscope to see what opportunities and dangers are coming up ahead, while the ship's company keep her on course. He depends on the knowledge of his engineer and radar officer to help him to interpret what he sees, and to draw up his strategy for the next move. The speed of decision-making and complexity of equipment make it impossible for him to know everything himself, he is constantly learning from his subordinates.

It is no different for other managers. Constant change throws up new complexities and problems almost daily. Past experience is not always still relevant, new solutions are needed, and managers do not have all the answers. It is not only specialised knowledge which a manager can learn from his or her subordinates, but fresh ways of tackling problems by those who are dealing with them. Neither can managers hope to cope singlehanded with the information explosion in our high-tec society.

The subordinates you can learn from may come from anywhere down the line. If you are in a fast-moving, high-tec industry, learn from those who have the latest technical knowledge – and that may be a young graduate still wet behind the ears and pretty low down the pecking order.

If you have transferred from one organisation to another, or have been appointed to manage a discipline different to your own, the fastest and surest way to learn what you need to know about the system, the work, the people, is to ask your secretary and everybody else's secretaries! Being wise enough to know what it is you don't know, and having the confidence to ask someone who does, whether it's the chief engineer or the tea-lady, can prevent a new manager making a bad start, from which he may never quite recover.

> One new health board chief was hardly seen at all for several weeks after his appointment. Needless to say, fantasies and rumours about the new boss were rife. When he did eventually emerge from his office, it was to instruct his secretary to type an edict to all medical staff enclosing a brand new form for controlling the indent and distribution of medical supplies. His subsequent embarrassment would have been less if only he had asked someone; they would have told him that a similar system was already in use – the only difference was, it was better!

The growing tendency to appoint general managers, regardless of sector, which has gone along with the recognition of management as a discipline in itself, means that managers will increasingly have to learn from and consult people at all levels in the company if they want to survive. It may also be safer to learn from subordinates than to ask too many questions of your boss (that individual may still be wondering whether he or she has made the right appointment). Asking too much, too soon, from your new peer group also has its hazards, particularly in a highly competitive environment.

Apart from self-interest, there are benefits in the development of staff too. They get recognition for the expertise they have, and teaching others is an excellent way of reinforcing and extending their own knowledge – particularly if you have done your homework sufficiently to know what to ask about, and what to do with it once you've been told. Asking intelligent and searching questions from a different viewpoint to that of subordinates can broaden their vision and give a new dimension to their task.

To make it work in a way that develops your subordinates at the same time as yourself, there are three important pre-conditions:

- You must first establish your competence as a manager in some other relevant field, so that your interest is seen as a genuine desire to learn about a specific area of work against a background of other knowledge and expertise. Otherwise staff may feel taken advantage of by someone they see as earning twice what they get and knowing half as much.

- There must already exist a good relationship of mutual trust between yourself and the subordinate. All forms of staff development depend on good basic relationships between bosses and subordinates. You should in any case pick the person you are going to learn from carefully. Chat to the personnel department first, though, and find out who it was in your department applied for your job but didn't get it. You'd better wait a while before picking those brains!

- It is not a good idea to seek tuition from your subordinates from a position of complete ignorance. You must do some homework -enough to know exactly what it is you want to learn, why, and what you can do with it. This is not the occasion to ask the 'idiot' question which is supposed to produce insight in the recipient; it will be seen too readily for what it is.

Be careful not to develop 'favourites' in your team to whom you invariably go for information that others could just as easily give you. It could damage the balance of good relationships. Spread the benefits of two-way learning as evenly as you can throughout your team. They will soon recognise that you value learning, know where to get it from, and how to use it. It is a good example to them that asking and learning is 'okay'.

42

Create a Learning Environment

No matter how ripe the seed, how carefully the weeds are pulled or the ground is watered, if it is sown on barren and unyielding soil it will not flourish. So it is with the seeds of learning.

The efforts of trainers, managers and employees themselves towards human resource development are largely wasted if the culture of the organisation does not value its people and their development. Such an attitude is the more unfortunate, since the changes which are inevitably taking place – more complex technology, smaller and more flexible structures, the coordination of effort as far as information will reach, and new interpretations of employment – will all make the development of human resources even more vital to survival in both public and private sectors.

Any successful organisation has developed an image for itself. Think of the bank that 'listens', the quality product that never fails, the best value - 'If you find the same goods for a lower price anywhere else, we will refund the difference'.

Millions of pounds are spent not only on creating but maintaining that image. Where competition is really keen, a product is only as good as its latest advertising campaign. But what is the image inside your organisation? What do your employees know you for? Do they get listened to? Get quality management? Receive good value for their efforts? Have they tried and abandoned the idea of improvement and advancement because 'It doesn't get you anywhere around here'?

Learning is not an activity divorced from work. Developing employee potential is part of the reality of management in the here and now – in the way we think, plan, act and organise.

To assess whether your organisation operates in a learning environment, consider the following questions:

● How often and by whom is training and development talked about in your department, in the canteen, in the boardroom, on the shop-floor? It's a sure sign of how important something is.

- Do your subordinates expect to undertake regular development activities, or would they view it as an aberration on your part or as a not-so-veiled personal criticism?

- Is the idea of training and development accepted as a matter of course by your boss? By the unions?

- Are the training specialists in your organisation participants in corporate strategy and goal formulation? Are they even kept informed on planning and strategic issues?

- When you're busy, is someone's training course the first thing to be cancelled, or the training budget the first thing to be cut?

- Do you tell your customers and clients that training is important to you, e.g. by telling them what training you do, by having trainees wearing badges to announce the fact, by a notice explaining a change in opening/servicing hours 'to allow for training'?

- Do you outline the importance and availability of training and development in your recruitment literature, and during induction procedures?

- How does your organisation view people with ambition and drive – as a threat? Does it promote only clones of the smooth 'round-peg-who-won't-rock-the-boat' category?

- Does your organisation positively encourage creative, innovative, challenging ideas, and risk-taking? Do you support people, champion their ideas – even when they're a pain in the neck?

- Do you assume that people will learn from their experience, or are steps taken to ensure the learning is made explicit, applied and appraised?

- Is development and performance rewarded – by merit payments, bonuses, up-grading, promotion, a trip to Hawaii?

- Is learning rewarded – by recognition, feedback, responsibility, more learning opportunities?

- What is your attitude towards the training specialists in the organisation? How much interest do you show in their effectiveness? When were you last in the training department? When were their staff last on your patch? Do they attend your departmental meetings from time to time? Do you share with them what you are trying to achieve?

- How thoroughly do you investigate lack of success at courses or study programmes by your staff? Do you brief them and debrief them before and after training activities?

- When employees resign, are they interviewed to find out why? And does anyone listen to them?

- How often do training and development items appear in your house journal, news bulletin, annual report?

- Does your organisation operate on rigid job descriptions or do people have jobs in which there is scope for developing both the job and themselves, where they can initiate and participate in the change?

- Do you try to train poor performers without asking whether they are in the right jobs, or do you view job/person/environment as part of the same equation in obtaining optimum results?

Social and technological changes are beginning to demand new kinds of structures – more organic and flexible organisations which can not only adapt to change but have the capacity for pro-active change. This will only be possible in organisations capable of learning, by the constant process of questioning and listening, to both customers and employees. To a learning organisation, training and development are not optional extras but part of working life – an essential part of its ethos.

43

Evaluate Training and Development

Faith, hope and charity may be important virtues but they are not enough to persuade most chief executives of the need to maintain the training and development department when the axe is being wielded. Neither should they be enough to convince you that your own staff development activities are effective.

Evaluation of off-the-job training courses includes an assessment of the relevance and content of the course material and the teaching methods, as well as the amount of learning by participants. Where specific skills and knowledge are concerned, measurement is fairly straightforward if practical and written tests are well designed and properly interpreted. Questionnaires, discussion groups and individual interviews are also used to evaluate responses to training.

But even in off-the-job courses, the line manager has a vital part to play in assessing the return on investment in time, money and effort. The first problem is that unless the objectives in sending an individual on a course are clearly known, i.e. exactly what knowledge, skill or behavioural change is being sought, then it is impossible to measure whether it has been achieved. It is also difficult to know whether the right type of course has been selected. Second, the purpose of training and development is enhanced performance now and/or in the future, and this requires managerial assessment at the workplace, perhaps for an extended period.

The identification of training needs, the establishment of objectives, and assessment of performance back at work are primarily functions of line managers in conjunction with their staff, although close co-operation with the training professionals at each stage is likely to be rewarding to all concerned.

Next time you decide to send one of your staff on a course, whether it is run by your organisation's own training department or an outside provider, discuss your objectives with the training staff beforehand, and ask how the training will be evaluated, both during the course and for longer-term effects on performance. The stumbling block to effective evaluation is often line managers who think training is nothing to do with them and don't recognise their responsibility in the assessment process. Your approach and co-operation will be welcomed by competent trainers – they want good and lasting results as much as you do. Trainers also want to quantify it where possible and spread it around – their job may depend on it.

Sophisticated methods of evaluation, which might include detailed interviewing, psychological testing for attitude change, return visits by participants or extensive surveys, can be expensive and are obviously justifiable only in the case of large and costly training programmes. Less formal, though sometimes less objective, methods are more appropriate in many cases, particularly if it is difficult to put a monetary value on the results.

It may be possible to assess improvements in performance by measuring the change in the number of complaints, the error rate, wastage levels, increased sales, or output figures. The influence of such other factors as quality of materials, pressure of work, and co-workers have to be allowed for in the design of the evaluation, and accurate records must be maintained to enable before and after comparisons to be made.

But the development of personal and managerial skills, such as handling people, problem-solving, leadership or the ability to take initiative and hold responsibility, are far more difficult to measure and may be impossible to quantify in isolation. These are the skills in which your own staff development activities as the boss are vital, and there are good reasons why you should evaluate how effective your methods are:

- You can assess which approaches and activities are most effective for particular individuals.
- It enables other learning needs to be identified, and appropriate methods to be determined.
- It indicates where your own time and effort are giving the best results.
- It assesses your own strengths and weaknesses in staff development skills.
- The evaluation process can reinforce learning and expectations.
- It provides everyone with the satisfaction of knowing that staff development is effective (especially your boss, who may need a little convincing about some of the suggestions in this book, but once converted may give you better development opportunities too).

Evaluation begins with knowing where you want to get to, i.e. the skills you want to develop in an individual, or the behaviour you wish to encourage/discourage. Depending on the objectives, a number of evaluation methods can be used – it is more effective to use as many as possible at different times.

Reaction

After a coaching session, a temporary promotion, an action learning project, or other development experience, sit down with the trainees and ask how they feel about the experience as a method of development, how much they learned, whether it was the right method for them, and whether their own objectives have been met.

Observation
After a period of development in interview skills, verbal presentation, team briefing, or handling customers, observe your subordinates use these skills in their work. Note the activities in which they still have difficulties and discuss with them afterwards why this is so, and what other development' training on or off the job might help.

Testing/simulation
During and/or after a programme of development, get your subordinates to act out the skills or behaviour in a simulated situation (i.e. if there is too much risk in doing it for real), or by giving a written or verbal presentation of what has been learned. Discuss the results afterwards and listen carefully to their comments about how they learned and what they found most effective. If necessary, ask probing questions to get them to think about this aspect as well as the standard of their performance in the test.

Interview
A good boss will expose his or her subordinates to a range of development opportunities. At regular intervals, set aside time to have a quiet discussion with each person specifically on the methods they are finding most effective in their general development, including their response to your own coaching and delegating abilities. It is also a good time to up-date their personal development plan. This is not an appraisal interview. Performance is a part of it, but the focus of discussion should be the value of the development opportunities and methods being used to achieve your joint objectives in developing that individual.

Instruments
There is a range of questionnaires based on psychometric testing methods for measuring attitudes to work, personal priorities, management style, methods of handling conflict, stress levels and almost any other behaviour. Used at intervals of, say, 6 months, they can also measure changes. It is not always possible to identify what exactly has caused the change; there will be other factors than your staff development activities to take into account, but it does indicate if the individual is progressing in the desired direction to the satisfaction of you both.

It is necessary to be a licensed user for most of these instruments, which are usually copyright anyway. They also require some degree of expertise in their interpretation; in the hands of a novice they can be damaging. Even if you have experienced these on training courses yourself, resist the temptation to use them on others unless you are trained to do so. Consult the training staff in your company if you think this kind of evaluation would be useful for your team.

Results
Where these are quantifiable, e.g. reductions in errors, complaints, increases in output, etc., bear in mind earlier comments about the need to have accurate data for before and after analysis. The discussion of results should focus on what activities were most/least effective in achieving learning and influencing performance.

Effects on others
These can be assessed by general observation and measurement of performance and relationships within the section or department. It is more difficult to isolate the effects of specific forms of staff development, but group discussion focused on this issue is likely to produce some useful data to be used in conjunction with other evaluation methods.

These evaluation methods vary in formality and objectivity. Advice can be sought from training professionals, but ultimately it is a matter of your own judgement as to when each is most appropriate. But to be effective, it is important to make sure that the evaluation process does not merge with such other activities as coaching, giving feedback and performance appraisal. The prime purpose and focus of each of the methods described above must be the following:

- assessing how well the learning/development objectives have been achieved, in terms of time taken as well as resulting performance
- identifying the development methods which have been most effective for that individual
- the quality of your own activities in staff development, e.g. coaching, delegating, your skills in identifying development needs, and choice of methods to meet them.

The final stage of evaluation is updating and implementing your own development plan.

Resources
Effective evaluation is a constant problem for professional trainers, to which no easy answer has been found, and most literature on the subject is rather esoteric. But look at *Evaluating Training* by Peter Brawley (CIPD)

44

Manage Stress

Financial losses to UK industry from stress-related illness have been estimated at over £3,000 million a year by the Stress Syndrome Foundation. It is fast becoming the major industrial disease of our time, causing not only high absence rates from sickness but long-term debility and early death.

Some occupations have inherently higher stress potential than others. The following examples are drawn from a 'stress league' compiled for the Sunday Times by Cary Cooper, Professor of Organisational Psychology at the Manchester Institute of Science and Technology. The ratings are from 10 (the highest stress potential) to 0.

Miner (highest quoted)	8.3	Civil servant	4.4
Police	7.7	Accountant	4.3
Advertising	7.3	Engineer	4.3
Dentist	7.3	Local government officer	4.3
Taxman	6.8	Secretary	4.3
Nurse, midwife	6.5	Architect	4.0
Personnel	6.0	Lab technician	3.8
Manager (commerce)	5.8	Banker	3.7
Salesman, shop assistant	5.7	Computing	3.7
Stockbroker	5.5	Librarian (lowest quoted)	2.0

You may know people who thrive on pressure – produce their best results against tight deadlines, are in their element working all hours, and preferably on several different jobs at the same time. A certain amount of pressure is a good thing, it keeps us alert and stimulated, but for each of us there is an optimum level at which we give of our best. Beyond that (or indeed below it) we can suffer physically and psychologically from stress and strain.

People who operate well and healthily in high-pressure jobs are those with a high threshold for pressure. The danger is that this can vary with age, state of general health and other events happening in social and family life. No one is immune from the effects of stress if it is not recognised and managed at an early stage. Working in an environment which is constantly below one's pressure optimum can also lead to similar results, e.g. simply not having enough to do, or doing tasks which do not fully use abilities and skills.

The basis of managing stress is maintaining this optimum pressure balance against constant changes in biological, social and environmental factors, over many of which we have no direct control. In this area more than any other, it becomes essential to recognise that employees are whole people, incorporating social and psychological needs, and not just animated work stations. Potential sources of stress – major life changes, personality/early experiences, and factors inherent in the job – are all interrelated and can potentiate and spill over into each other. Work stress may result in someone going home and kicking the cat or throwing the television at the kids; home stress can equally lead to bad judgement or fatal error at work.

Life changes, such as bereavement, divorce, and physical illness or injury are all known to be potential causes of stress. But even supposedly pleasant events like getting married, starting a new job, buying a bigger house and having a new addition to the family all increase pressure levels. The effect on each person will depend on what other stressors they are subject to at the time, their general health, their stress threshold, their skill at managing stress and the support or otherwise of those around them – including their boss.

Personality and previous experiences can create stressors which are very individual. For some people, speaking in public is a major source of stress, producing physical symptoms of dry mouth, wobbly kneecaps and sweaty palms. For others it may be flying, receiving criticism, going to the boss's boss, or not managing to avoid the person they most dislike when going for lunch in the canteen.

High levels of stress are often found in dangerous or insecure jobs, those that have tight deadlines or erratic worldoads, or where there is little margin for error. Other stressful jobs include those with a high level of competitiveness or potential conflict, responsibility for controlling the behaviour of others or dealing with other's problems and emotions, or jobs where working relations are poor, particularly those with superiors.

The following are some of the more common symptoms of stress which managers attending various stress workshops have described to me:

- **Physical**: aches and pains, especially in head, neck and back; dry mouth; sweaty palms; increased heart beat; nausea; indigestion; fatigue; agitation; insomnia; blurred vision; cramps; tremor; proneness to minor illnesses; heart attack; waking up tired.
- **Psychological**: anxiety; confusion; withdrawal; emotionality, e.g. excessive feelings of anger, tearfulness, helplessness, frustration; lack of concentration; irrational fear; depression.

- **Behavioural**: irritability; over/under eating; increase in alcohol; increase in smoking; mistakes; obsessive activities; repetitive actions; poor judgement; absenteeism; bad time-keeping; working excessive hours; accidents; blaming others; blaming self, mood changes; forgetfulness; loss of humour.

Many of the symptoms seem contradictory, because individuals' responses vary widely. The most important indicator is probably a change from normal behaviour, e.g. someone who is normally punctilious about time and detail becoming sloppy, or the casual individual suddenly becoming obsessive about minor matters.

The list is not exhaustive, and of course there may be a number of causes in any one instance other than stress. This is one of the problems in early diagnosis – symptoms are explained away and nothing is done to relieve the excessive pressure until it is too late. One of the most important questions you, as a boss, can ask when noticing behavioural changes in your staff is 'Could he or she be suffering from stress?'

The body's automatic and combined physical/psychological response to stress is a healthy and essential survival mechanism. In the days when we lived among dinosaurs, this response sent chemicals flooding into the bloodstream, and the resultant physiological changes prepared us to fight (with the possibility of brontosaurus burgers for supper) or to run like hell (properly called the fight/flight syndrome).

Our physiology has not changed, and when we come up against any situation we perceive as a threat, the same chemicals are produced. Unfortunately on most occasions we can neither take flight nor sock the boss on the jaw, so we have to stay and stew in our own juice. It is when the body is in this constrained 'ready state' too often or for too long a period that the damage is done. Managing stress is not aimed at stopping the 'alarm reaction' but at regaining a 'steady state' as soon as possible after it occurs, and reducing the number of alarm signals we receive by adjusting the environment.

What is the boss's role in all this? Employees who are under too much pressure from whatever source do not perform well, and they are certainly not amenable to development. But apart from controlling work stress to ensure optimum performance and to enable staff development to take place, stress management is possible as a form of development in itself, to help your subordinates control their pressure levels and increase their stress threshold.

The first stage is to ask yourself 'Do I cause stress to my subordinates?' Junior and middle managers tend to suffer more from work-related stress than senior and top managers, and one of the reasons is the way they are managed by their bosses. The following are some of the major reasons given by middle managers for experiencing excessive pressure:

- Feeling unable to influence my immediate superior's decisions when they directly affect me.
- Not having sufficient information/authority/autonomy to carry out responsibilities assigned to me.
- Feeling I have too heavy a workload ever to be able to complete it properly.
- Thinking I can't satisfy the conflicting demands of various people over me.
- Being unclear about the scope/responsibilities/objectives of my job.
- Not knowing quite what is expected of me or what my boss thinks of my performance.
- Not knowing what opportunities there are for advancement.
- Feeling I'm not fully qualified to handle myself in the job.
- Not getting enough encouragement or support from my superiors.
- Not hitting it off with my boss.

Note how many of these sources of stress relate to feelings of uncertainty and powerlessness. If any of these statements could be made by your subordinates, miss a turn, go back to Chapter 1 and spend a couple of evenings critically reviewing how, or even if, you develop your staff.

Even if you are not causing stress in any of these ways, there are a lot of other steps you can take to create an environment in which you and your team can learn to identify and work within your optimum pressure levels most of the time:

☑ Establish a positive attitude towards stress in the workplace. Point out that it is neither a status symbol to be worn like a badge of honour nor a sign of weakness. Have it known that you view it as an element of the job which has to be managed and controlled for everyone's benefit.

☑ Be on the look-out for early signs of what may be stress symptoms, and encourage others to do so.

☑ Maintain regular face-to-face contact with your staff so that you can pick up early problems and they have a chance to talk to you informally.

☑ Do an audit on the way you manage your department and the way your subordinates manage their people. Take steps to reduce obvious potential stressors wherever possible, whether or not there are existing signs of stress.

☑ Give all those who report to you as much autonomy and real control over their work and conditions as possible – don't just accept the status quo. Rethink job descriptions and functions if necessary.

☑ Arrange training sessions on stress management, and follow them up with team meetings on how stress levels can be reduced at work.

☑ Review your own time-management, train your staff to improve theirs, and give regular encouragement to keep it up – it is the one management technique seeming to need constant reinforcement.

☑ Arrange for the local general practitioner, dietician or clinical psychologist to run discussion groups in work time on health, exercise, diet and relaxation. All these can increase resistance to the effects of stress.

☑ Have your staff learn a 5-minute relaxation routine and encourage them to use it during the day when they feel under pressure, angry, or frustrated. This 5 minutes could save hours or days if it prevents a bad decision.

☑ Never try to continue a discussion/interview with people who are angry or in any other way highly emotional, but give them an opportunity to calm down first. They won't be listening to you in that state anyway.

☑ Be ready to offer counselling to staff who may need it. If doing so yourself, be alert to when you should offer professional counselling from outside.

☑ Encourage regular exercise – have works keep-fit sessions, fun-runs, walks. If you think you can get away with it, follow the Japanese and set up morning exercise before work starts. Set an example even if it hurts and you can't find a track suit that fits anymore. (Anyone taking up unaccustomed rigorous exercise should first take medical advice on their intentions.)

☑ Insist that everyone takes break times, lunches, rest days, and holiday entitlement (including you).

☑ Ensure the best possible job/people match, and discuss changes where necessary.

☑ Be flexible and supportive if any of your subordinates need help in managing stress from outside work, e.g. temporary change/relief from high pressure/high risk work, adjustment in hours, time to visit helping agencies etc.

☑ Reduce levels of uncertainty by ensuring employee communications are effective, particularly in relation to imminent changes in structure or conditions.

☑ Take a look at the menu in the canteen – if it offers only chip 'butties' and bangers, negotiate more variety. It doesn't have to be all soya beans and bran, but if the firm is providing a food service, it might at least offer meals that will help keep the staff alive and at work.

☑ Phase changes, don't change everything at once, and give people a chance to adapt and to participate.

☑ Watch your own stress levels, diet, exercise and relaxation. Stress is highly contagious – and not only for the cat!

Having got this far, if you are aware of a gentle throbbing in the temple and your palms feel sticky, take a walk around the block, come back and relax completely for five minutes before working out all the things you ought to be doing about it!

Resources

A very useable book which looks at all aspects of employee wellness, including dealing with stress and other negative influences, is *Creating an Employee Wellness Programme*, by Laurel Alexander, Management Books 2000.

A useful book that helps executives and managers to identify and deal with stress in others within their organisation is Dr Vernon Coleman's *Stress Management Techniques 2nd Edition*, published by Management Books 2000.

45

Command Your Time

There is no such thing as not having enough time – only not having enough commitment. Time is a great leveller. We all get the same amount of this precious and perishable commodity – not even the chief executive can wangle 25 hours in the day. The great differentiator is how we use it.

Many managers, especially those new to the function, feel more comfortable at the operational level with work they know they do well. They work long and hard and may get results (in the short term), but they are results their subordinates could and should be producing while they concentrate on managing.

It is not easy to convince these overworked managers that they are not short of time, but they are expending it on the wrong activities. Getting command of your time is not about doing more, faster (which can waste time as a result of stress, fatigue and error); it is about doing the right things.

Developing and training subordinates is a time-consuming activity, but it is not an optional extra. It is the basis of effective management and good results, and is therefore one of the 'right things' for which time should be managed. -

Managing time effectively is not something you can do entirely on your own. Others have a legitimate call on your attention – subordinates, customers, the boss, the chairman – but there are many illegitimate users of your time too! If you intend to start a new regime of time-management, then you must gain the co-operation of your boss, colleagues, subordinates and especially your secretary. Without their co-operation you will not succeed and may run the risk of having your 'unavailability' misunderstood.

Start with some short training sessions with your team. Share with them the methods and priorities you intend to adopt and encourage them to do the same in improving their use of time – both their own and yours.

There are plenty of courses, videos and books about time-management, so let's concentrate on suggestions which are dual purpose, i.e. they will help you use time more effectively to do the things that really matter, while at the same time developing your staff.

The basic requirement is to know what you are aiming at – if you don't know where you're going it doesn't much matter when, or if, you get there. The objectives must be clear, so that the priorities which enable you to achieve them can be identified. Break down the priorities into key tasks and determine which ones only you personally could, or should, do – these are the 'right things' to which you need to allocate your time.

The three basic methods for doing this are time-saving, work-shedding, and time-budgeting.

The biggest **time-saving** can be in reducing interruptions to your day. Fifty interruptions a week, each of 6 minutes, amounts to 5 hours and a lot of breaks in concentration. If you have an 'open door' policy, which in practice means that your office is a control-free zone all day, then everyone else's priorities are running you, not yours. If your job requires you to be available at any time for certain key people – clients, the chief executive, safety control officer – then it is even more important for non-priority interrupters to be controlled.

The door should be open to give complete access, especially to your subordinates, for certain definite periods. Subordinates can save up queries they want to raise with you and deal with them in one session. The chances are they will have solved most of the problems themselves in the meantime anyway. They will also learn to make better use of the time they do have with you, ensuring they have all the data, have defined the problem clearly, and are really sure it is a problem that should come to you. The more you value your time and are seen to do so, the more others will value it too.

Encourage your subordinates to have 'closed' times, perhaps a couple of hours in the morning when they do not interrupt each other (and you don't interrupt them either unless it is really necessary), and 'open' times when they freely interact. The 'closed' times should coincide with the period of the day when people are at their personal best, or when lengthy, complex or particularly important tasks, or tasks requiring a lot of concentration, are undertaken.

If you get a lot of interruptions from staff on their work, especially tasks you have delegated, set aside some time to review the way you delegate to them, reassess their training needs, or consider whether you initiate enough contact with them yourself in giving feedback and general attention. Staff who are neglected sometimes use work queries as a way of getting the attention and recognition they need, and it is likely to be at times or with a frequency that causes unnecessary interruptions for you. Plan sufficient contact time with subordinates at times when it suits your own priorities.

If you don't have a system which enables all telephone calls to be filtered by your secretary, negotiate for one. Share with your secretary your daily priorities of tasks and people so that he or she can work along with you in controlling interruptions. This sharing will give a clearer view of the secretary's own objectives as well as enlisting commitment to yours.

Never take calls on work you have delegated to someone else. If the task has some connection with others in the organisation, then they should already have been told to whom the task has been delegated. If they have come straight to you, it is probably to take a short-cut, ask a favour, or because they are too status-conscious to talk to a subordinate. Either way, you will undermine the authority you have given your subordinate to do the job if you interfere by accepting the call. Brief your secretary on who is dealing with what, and let her divert the caller to the right quarter. They may even learn from your example of delegation. The only exception to this is if the caller is registering a major complaint about the delegated work which you ought to know about – but that is part of briefing your secretary.

Handle each piece of paper only once. Don't play patience with the correspondence half the morning, trying to decide what to do with it. Set aside a time for mail. Look at it alongside your development plans for subordinates and your own task list, and unless it is essential that only you do it, or you have left it beyond a deadline, delegate it. There are only three options to choose from – do it yourself, delegate it, or put it in the bin – do, delegate or dump!

Work-shedding is mostly achieved through delegating. Chapter 8 explains how to do it in a developmental way, but the essentials in doing it in a way which also saves your time are as follows:

- ☑ Ensure the subordinate has the ability, information and resources necessary to do the job, or knows where to get them.
- ☑ Agree required results and standards.
- ☑ Arrange method and timing of reporting back to you (confirm how often you are available in the meantime if really necessary).
- ☑ Give them the power and authority to carry out the job and let everyone concerned know about it.
- ☑ Delegate as a means of developing the subordinate through work for which you are responsible but need not do personally – not as a way of clearing your desk on a Friday night.

Unnecessary work can also be shed by differentiating between perfection and excellence. Excellence is the consistent achievement of the right objectives in the most effective way. Perfection is usually a personal vanity, which goes beyond the objective and uses up time which should be spent on other priorities. Pride in a job comes from achieving all the tasks, not achieving some of them with more precision than is necessary. There can be little pride in achieving 30 per cent with perfection and leaving 70 per cent undone, when the objective is 100 per cent to an agreed standard.

A report needs to be clear, concise and accurate – not a contender for the Booker Prize. If subordinates are clear on objectives and standards, and can see when they have been achieved, they are more likely to gain satisfaction from achieving them, rather than their own personal goals which may be at the expense of the company's.

The third method of time-management is **time-planning or time-budgeting**. This requires quite an investment of time in itself, because it starts with keeping a detailed log of how you use time. Like money, unless you know what it is being spent on, it is difficult to determine where you can save it, and invest it more effectively.

Many people use a day planner or 'jobs to do' list. To be effective this should include priorities, i.e. 'must do', 'could do'. It should also include a large 'delegate to' column. Unfortunately, listing can sometimes become an alternative to doing, unless the daily planner is part of a longer-term time/work strategy; neither does a daily plan help to develop the capacity to allocate time more accurately and give attention to longer-term priorities – such as staff development.

The steps to be followed in real time-budgeting are to determine priorities, identify key tasks, allocate time to specific activities in a forward planner for up to about four weeks (or longer if the time-scale of your job requires it), and then keep a careful log of actual time spent and activities completed. Compare this to the plan until you learn to budget more accurately. Thereafter, only occasional logging will be necessary, just to ensure you are keeping up your budgeting standards.

Enlist your secretary's help in your planning, and don't fill out every time slot with tasks. Allow at least 20-30 per cent flexibility for crises, priority interrupters, and contingency planning. Time for the open-door period, management by walking about, coaching and feedback should all be allowed for in the plan.

This method can be applied to different areas of work. For example, if you are concerned that you may not be spending enough time on key tasks, plan time against these tasks and log what you spend time on each day, i.e. the actual activities you are engaged in and for how long. If you want to spend the right proportion of time on site, in the factory, or walking about as opposed to time working in the office or at home, plan time for work in specific places and log where you work. The same can be done by planning time to allow for necessary or acceptable interruptions, and then recording when, for how long and by whom, you are interrupted each day. But a useful log for staff development is to decide how much time you should be spending with each subordinate over the next month. Budget the time for it, then record who you see and for how long, and check it against the plan. Simply by logging these contacts in the first place, you may discover that you have divided your team into 'favourites' and 'neglecteds', or that you have not spent more than five minutes at a time with any one person during the last two weeks.

Building effective relationships and developing skills requires more than fleeting contact, however frequent or constructive. It takes larger chunks of time to get to understand people, communicate values, enlist commitment, and reach a position where you share goals.

A contacts planner and log can also be useful for ensuring that you are spending enough time with your boss, with customers, and in networking with colleagues. Contacts grow weak if they are not nurtured with regular doses of time.

Time-management is one of those ideas which seem excellent at the time, and you can't understand why you haven't done all these activities before – they are all so obvious really. The answer is probably that you have, several times. But time is abstract and elusive, whereas interruptors, side-tracks and temptations are concrete and constantly present. To maintain your good intentions, it is essential to review progress and reinforce your methods regularly. Budget time at least every 6 months for a team meeting specifically to review how time is being spent and where it could be used more effectively. Bad habits can be corrected, any problems arising from times or length of open/closed periods can be discussed and resolved, and good ideas which anyone has for saving time on jobs can be shared to mutual benefit.

Your objective should be to manage the most scarce resource – time – to enable you to develop the most valuable resource – people.

Resources

Barrie Pearson's *Common Sense Time Management* is a good book for tightening up your personal time controls - Management Books 2000.

46

Develop Yourself

In early times in Japan, bamboo-and-paper lanterns were used with candles inside.

> A blind man, visiting a friend one night, was offered a lantern to carry home with him. 'I do not need a lantern', he said. 'Darkness or light is all the same to me.'
>   'I know you do not need a lantern to find your way', his friend replied, 'but if you don't have one, someone else may run into you. So you must take it.'
> The blind man started off with the lantern and before he had walked very far someone ran squarely into him. 'Look where you are going! ' he exclaimed to the stranger. 'Can't you see this lantern?'
>   'Your candle has burned out, brother', replied the stranger.

Experienced managers who have been around long enough to feel that training and development is not for them, but will nonetheless encourage it for their staff, may need some stimulus from outside before they realise that their own candle may need relighting. During training programmes, the most frequent comment from participants, ranging from junior to senior managers, is 'That's all very well, but you should have my boss on this programme too!'

Recognising a need for self-development doesn't mean you are a bad manager. It shows an appreciation that even the best managers need to be stretched and stimulated if they are to remain adaptive, alert and motivated. This has never been more true than in our present society, with unprecedented rates of change affecting every facet of our lives. One area in particular in which we can all learn and grow at any stage in life, if we have a mind to, is in understanding and coping with ourselves and others – the stock in trade of a manager.

Development is not something we can just do to other people. We can't develop others unless we also share in the process of learning and show an example of development. I have met many bosses whose ideas on what training blithely at every course. In practice, it is unrealistic to expect anyone to be able to sit down and just answer them. The questioning is a development process in itself and should not be rushed, nor attempted in isolation. Below are some suggestions of activities you can undertake which themselves are developmental, but which can be used primarily to start this questioning process. Ideally you will throw out the questions quoted above and construct your own, but the questioning and answering will begin to take place simultaneously as you go through the various activities. By the time you draw up your plan, you may already have started some of the things you want to develop, and the plan will need constantly adjusting and developing with experience. Your commitment is to action, but you're free to change your mind on the content – it's your plan!

● Make a contract with yourself by noting down the main reasons why you intend to concentrate on self-development.

● Every chapter in this book could equally apply to your own development as to that of your staff. Look again through the chapters which most interest you, and do a 'learning log' after each chapter, i.e. note down the things in it that were most important to you, list what you learned from this, what actions you intend to take as a result, what else you need to know to take the action, and how/where/when you can learn it.

● Do a 'learning log' after significant experiences – a particularly important meeting; handling a tough situation; prolonged personal contact such as an appraisal, counselling or interview session; or working through a knotty problem. The review process not only helps you to learn from the experience itself, but helps identify where further learning or experience is needed; and you could build that need into your plan.

● Pick a few people you trust and ask them for feedback on various aspects of your performance and/or personal behaviour.

● Think over the last time you were appraised by your boss. If you don't have that system, ask him or her for an opportunity to discuss your progress, and share with your boss as much of your development intentions as you feel able to, and encourage feedback.

● Brainstorm with yourself to identify new work experiences you might try if you took a week out of work. Select one, and arrange a week out to do it within the next six months – even if you have to use some annual leave.

● Brainstorm with your team what things you would all like to see change in your section. Include aspects of each other's behaviour in the exercise (yours too). Keep it a light and humorous event – the person asked to make the most personal changes can win a bottle of wine – but listen out for true words spoken in jest, and if appropriate, follow up with a quiet chat in private to get a little more feedback. You have to be able to listen without being defensive to do this, and to have a reasonably good relationship so that you can trust each other to be honest when asked, without recrimination.

● Join an action learning set. Commit yourself to the group and learn from the listening and questioning within the set how they see you.

Not all these suggestions will work for everyone. What you find appropriate and helpful will depend on you, but if you find yourself rejecting any one of them out of hand as being quite abhorrent, probe a little deeper and ask yourself why. This could be one of your first really good questions.

Resources

As mentioned before, *Build Your Own Rainbow* by Hopson and Scally is excellent here. See also *Maximise Your Potential* by Ian Seymour. Both are published by Management Books 2000.

47

Image Build

One of those proverbial truisms we absorb without really knowing where it came from is the expression 'Justice must be seen to be done'. It is based on the very sound principle that the only reality is what people perceive. Perception depends to a large extent on each person's feelings, attitudes and experiences, through which they interpret what their senses tell them. But it also depends on the visibility and quality of the messages they receive. Whatever our beliefs about the value of people and developing them at work, and however sincerely we talk about it, unless we ensure that what we do and the way in which we do it enables others to perceive our intentions correctly, they will not be real as far as others are concerned.

It is not that we should be blowing our own trumpets all the time. Though talking about them is important, it is our actions and symbols which communicate to those around us what we are trying to achieve and what we believe.

The hallmark of an effective leader is the ability to operate simultaneously at the level of abstract ideas, vision, values, and everyday action, sometimes in minute detail. The leader needs to be able to demonstrate what is valued through frequent everyday actions in a way which makes them clear to his or her own team, to everyone else's team, and indeed to the customers and clients outside. The kind of questions a boss should ask are 'Does my team know what I am proud of?' 'What am I known for?' 'What do my team, and others in the organisation associate me with?'

You create the reputation not only for yourself but for your team, in the rest of the organisation and outside it. This can determine the environment in which they have to work and develop.

One boss had a long history of resentment about missing a senior post, and expressed it in certain personality clashes with heads of other departments. Gradually he acquired the reputation for being 'snappy' and erratic, and was not taken very seriously by senior colleagues. The effect on his staff was that they were often not taken seriously either, which limited the effectiveness of the whole department, especially where inter-departmental co-operation was necessary. They were discouraged from liaising with staff who reported to senior managers their boss particularly disliked, to the detriment of their own development and that of their work. Some of his subordinates attempted to work according to their own objectives without consulting the boss at all, and others simply gave up.

Your image as the boss also provides an example for your team to look up to, and perhaps emulate; and it certainly gives them cues as to what is valued and how to express it. They are the signs and symbols which indicate what you and your team stand for.

It can be a salutary lesson to see ourselves as others see us, and there is an amusing but very revealing exercise used with groups of management students when they have had a few days to work together in a mutually supportive atmosphere and can afford to be frank with each other. Each person writes down on a slip of paper the names of animals and the members of the group with which they associate each one. The fun is increased by the tutor listing on the board the animals only, and getting the class to guess which person it relates to, before revealing the original name. The ensuring discussion as to why the association is made can be both informative and therapeutic. The 'victim' each time is given the first opportunity to enter the discussion, and there is no chance of subsequent retaliation in picking associations, because they are all written down at the outset. Whether or not there is any consensus on each person's image, there is always a great deal to be learned by everybody from the discussion, which usually continues unabated in the bar.

If you have the courage, you could try this with your own team as a mutual awareness exercise. But it needs to be done in an atmosphere of trust and good humour. The fun is central to the learning – it usually is.

What would your team see you as? Perhaps they see you as a bear, tough and action-orientated, who defends the team but whose strengths lead you to dominate and encourage 'yes' men or women. Maybe they consider you a tortoise, dependable and consistent but likely to hold the team back in the race by pondering too long on problems and withdrawing into your shell when challenged? They may even liken you to a chameleon, quick, adaptable and versatile, but always likely to change unexpectedly.

Images are made not so much by what we say as what we do, especially to and with people, because it is their interpretation of our effect upon them which makes the image. Our actions generate the stories which express our values and create other people's expectations of us. Words we don't follow through with actions are soon recognised as hollow and are disregarded. Values have to be enacted, often and with impact.

☑ Establish little ceremonies to celebrate team achievements, or a milestone in an individual's work/career. Open a bottle of wine, award a plastic gnome – it doesn't matter what, as long as you share some fun and excitement about the achievements you value.

☑ Make successes known. If someone acquires a qualification or pulls of an important deal, write about it in the departmental newsletter. Better still, take a regular column in the company journal.

☑ Go and talk to people at their place of work instead of summoning them to your office. It is less intimidating, so they will respond better, and your visibility is higher.

☑ Network through the organisation on behalf of your team as well as yourself. Be aware of your role as ambassador in relation to your boss and the rest of the organisation. Set trails and open doors for your team to use in developing themselves and their work.

☑ Be loyal to your staff, even when they make mistakes. You can hold the post-mortem afterwards in private – preferably with constructive feedback rather than recriminations.

☑ Make the resources and time for staff development available, preserve them as a priority and make sure all your team know that. If you have had to fight hard to increase the training budget or get release for someone, share with them the problems you had and how you overcame them.

☑ Use your own time in helping staff develop, not just in giving feedback and coaching, but at a deeper level. Discuss with them an application to join a professional institute, go over a written course assignment with them, give them a 'mock' interview for practice or get a colleague to do so.

☑ Be demonstrably unselfish in the encouragement and assistance you give your staff in furthering their careers, even if it means you lose them from your team.

Ask yourself, 'Do I really believe in developing my staff?' If the answer is 'yes', does anybody else realise that? Do your subordinates? Their subordinates? Your boss?

If the answer is 'no', is management really the best career for you?

48

Manage Your Boss

How do you see your boss – as a boon or a burden? You may think by now that you have more than enough to do in developing your subordinates without taking on the responsibility of managing and developing your boss as well. But the fact is, it takes two to tango, and it is as much your job to create an effective working relationship with your boss as it is his or hers. If the relationship is poor, you must be at least half the problem. Once you realise that much, you can be more than half the solution.

We don't normally choose our bosses, any more than we choose our relatives. We may be able to avoid Uncle Arthur and Auntie Mildred except for the ritual exchange of socks and indigestion at Christmas time, but unless we want to make life hell for ourselves, damage the company, create difficulties for our subordinates, or move on, we must find a means of collaborating with our bosses that achieves their priorities as well our own in pursuit of organisational goals.

There are four important things to remember about bosses:

- They are human, i.e. they are not infallible and have the same needs and hang-ups as the rest of us.

- They are as dependent upon us as we are upon them. (It is a paradox that the higher up the hierarchy we move, and the more power and status we acquire, the more dependent we become on the information, integrity and effort of others.)

- They have different constraints, pressures and priorities than we have – it is never quite possible fully to appreciate the view from their window.

- They have bosses too.

Not only is it in your own interests to maintain an effective working relationship with the boss, but as a manager, you are also an ambassador for your subordinates both to your boss and to the rest of the organisation. Depending on your situation, the latter may only be possible through the good services of your immediate superior, and you are likely to need his or her support or at least approval in carrying out the following staff development activities:

- exchanges, secondments and action learning sets connecting with outside organisations
- changes in personnel policies regarding job descriptions, appraisal systems, recruitment, promotion procedures and other structures which are potential constraints upon staff development
- networking throughout the organisation as a means of opening doors for the benefit of yourself and your staff
- the acceptance of the kind of risk-taking and mistakes which permit experimentation, creativity and learning
- the establishment and/or increase of training budgets
- influencing the higher echelons on the importance of staff development and creation of a learning environment
- implementing your own development plans.

If you have already worked through the chapters on knowing yourself, identifying your strengths and weaknesses, and understanding how what you say and do influences the responses you get from others, you are already half way to working out how to relate effectively to your boss. This does not mean being a creep or a 'yes' man or woman, but complementing his or her strengths with your own, and recognising a boss's needs in the relationship too. But we must first know the person we would wish to influence. Do you know the answers to the following, and if so, do you use the information in managing the relationship with your boss?

- How does the boss like information – written for him or her to mull over, or face to face to allow for question and answer?
- How often and on what issues does the boss like you to make direct personal contact?
- How does the boss like to control what you do – before or after the event? Does he or she want only the bad news?
- What does your boss expect of you?
- How much does he or she know of your achievements?
- What are your boss's main strengths and weaknesses?
- What are your boss's priorities, values and goals?

When a new managing director took over a small manufacturing concern, his style was very different from his predecessor's. The previous boss had taken little direct interest in the day-to-day running of the business, especially anything to do with staffing. The heads of departments who were keen on training were able to do quite a bit without referring to him, but his lack of interest extended to lack of encouragement and resources too, and what they could achieve had to be done within the 'guidelines' of no cost, no change, and no disturbance. The new MD took a close interest in all staffing matters and started by asking for advance notice of attendance at courses, conferences and other development activities by staff within each department. One director resented what he interpreted as interference in an area of activity he had hitherto seen as his own domain, though within a pretty negative environment. Rather than inform his new boss about these activities, he either curtailed them or carried on without letting him know. The other directors adapted to the different style of the new MD, and soon found that he used the information on training and development to increase training resources, and encouraged them to undertake far more adventurous and innovative methods of development without interfering with how they were implemented.

You may argue that the new boss should have communicated more clearly his intentions in asking for information on training which previously had not been required – and so he should. But bosses are not infallible, remember; a perceptive subordinate will recognise this and realise that merely feeling righteous or resentful in response to a perceived wrong simply creates a vicious circle, resulting in a relationship which does nobody any good.

Most problems are opportunities yet to be managed and a difficult boss/subordinate relationship is no exception.

When it comes to influencing the boss, it is worth remembering that of the four major sources of power – expertise, personality, resources and status – it is only the latter one which the boss necessarily has more of than you do. In the others you may be stronger than your superiors, for the following reasons:

- **Expert power** comes from your specialised knowledge and skills, but it only has force if such expertise is known about and appreciated. So don't hide your light under a bushel – spread it around a bit, and keep up to date.

- **Personality power** depends primarily on the ability to handle people, and your innate charm. We can't all be charismatic, neither can we change our basic personalities, but we all have a lot of scope for improving interpersonal skills.

- **Resource power** includes information, and in the context of boss-management it also includes the performance and output of your section or department.

Using what you know about yourself, your boss, and your power base, you may influence your boss, in creating a learning environment and enabling you to pursue your staff development plans, in the following ways:

☑ Nothing succeeds like success, but only if the boss knows about it. Find ways to inform him or her of your people's achievements and your own with progress reports, demonstrations, presentations, etc.

☑ Check out with the boss that the staff development you propose is compatible with company culture and goals and demonstrate the link between the two.

☑ Encourage your boss to indulge in some personal development activity – talk about what other heads of department are doing, drop a leaflet on an interesting seminar at some exclusive venue renowned for its cuisine, or suggest he or she is missing out on something.

A company trainer who wanted to get the heads of departments away for a weekend seminar to demonstrate the benefits of a management development programme by giving them first-hand experience of it met with resistance during preliminary informal discussions. So he first launched the idea officially for their deputies, and when asked to approve the plans, the departmental heads decided unanimously that they should have the first bite of the cherry!

☑ Encourage your boss's interest in the development of your subordinates by getting him or her to give briefing sessions and talks, persuading him or her to attend and respond to presentations from your staff on some development experience they have just completed, or discussing with you the design of a training session.

☑ Discuss with the boss your personal development plans and ask for assistance. Be specific about the contribution you seek.

☑ Share with your boss regularly the results of your evaluation of training and development, but only if they are good. If they are not, improve your methods and results first.

☑ Promote the acceptance of exchanges, secondments and other external activities by highlighting spin-off to the company and to the boss personally – self-interest is very influential.

☑ Enlist your boss's support in creating contacts elsewhere in the organisation to assist your development activities, e.g. in forming project groups, arranging job rotations, or identifying suitable mentors.

☑ Leave this book lying around the office one Friday night, and when the boss comes up with ideas, let the boss think they are his/her own!

Resources

Despite the volume of material on managing subordinates, individuals and teams, the definitive and practical guide to boss-management has yet to be written!

49

Smile Often

Gorillas simply don't bring out the best in people. Because they look so fierce, man's response has been to run away or shoot them in fear.

In fact, gorillas are gentle and loving. They rarely fight, and the nearest they get to being really nasty is screaming angrily and rushing up to adversaries, coming to a sudden halt within inches of them, and staring them out – a bit like a pair of swaying, swearing drunks who don't have quite enough co-ordination left to take a swing at each other.

The showiness of the gorilla's aggression is a defence for their real cuddly natures. And so it is with many bosses. Some bosses frown all the time (1) because they don't realise they're doing it, (2) they are having a hard time thinking, or (3) because they need their eyes tested. But others do it on purpose: men because they think it gives them the kind of hard-nosed macho image that a boss ought to have, especially one who is 'in control' and going places; women because they feel they have to make up for the stereotype of the weaker sex and they want to give authority messages, and fear that a smile may be misinterpreted as a 'come-on'. In most cases it won't be if other verbal and non-verbal messages are clear. If the message is still misinterpreted, you would have had trouble whether you smiled or not, and other methods of making your position clear are called for.

Sales managers are always telling their counter staff to smile because it makes the customers feel important and appreciated. It also makes the sales assistant more approachable for information and advice about the product which could make the sale. But when the managers are talking to their subordinates, they often forget that the same applies to them.

Frowning and other aggressive behaviour either brings out the aggression in other people or it intimidates them. Whatever their reaction, you don't get much out of them, and you certainly don't develop them, because the results do not permit effective communication.

An unthreatening posture enables you to make contact with people more readily and to gain access to their listening and attention, so that they understand and are more willing to accept what you are trying to convey. Criticism and anger are more likely to generate a defensive denial and closing down of real communication.

Besides, if you go around the workplace with a habitual frown in the mistaken belief that this makes you look commanding, you practically have to jump up and down and foam at the mouth to show your disapproval. But the temporary removal of a usual smile can have a devastating effect on the recipient, who usually wishes to renew the more pleasurable status quo.

Smiling can have a wonderful effect on the morale of your team too. It makes people feel good about themselves and what they are doing. A smiling boss creates a positive and motivating atmosphere. Few people can resist smiling back. Even those fat, smiling Chinese Buddhas seen in the windows of antique shops make people smile. If you don't believe it, go inside the shop and watch the people looking into the window: it won't be the prices they're smiling at!

Smiling is not a sign of jovial weakness, it is an essential part of the body language of assertiveness. It indicates openness, confidence and acceptance of oneself and others around us. But it doesn't mean going around with a sickly grin all the time. That might make people suspicious, especially if they have read that line from Hamlet which goes 'one may smile, and smile, and be a villain'.

If you think there is nothing to smile about, your staff probably feel the same way too. Review the way you run your department and the kind of style and image you set, the enthusiasm you create. There is no management principle which says that work should not be fun. On the contrary, a sense of humour can turn negative, defeating attitudes into positive, winning ones, whatever line of business you may be in. Even undertakers have a sense of humour – although they have to be more careful with their sense of timing than most.

The important thing is to smile readily, frequently and naturally, to show that you feel good about the people who work for you. From the point of view of their development, it makes you more accessible to discuss problems and mistakes; they will be more willing to bring out their ideas and suggestions, and two-way listening and communication will be more effective. Learning from feedback places the learner in a vulnerable position. It is essential that they don't feel threatened. A smile confirms your good intentions and the positive nature of your comments. Your subordinates can relax, listen and benefit from the interaction.

It will also make you feel better, and help to reduce your stress level, if you smile more often. Not just at your subordinates but everyone you meet around the workplace – even the janitor. You might even encourage your boss to smile more often. But if the boss is already one of the world's smilers, it might be worth noting under what circumstances he or she smiles most – those who smile when things go wrong may have found someone to blame it on!

50

Be an Example

'Example is the school of mankind, and they will learn at no other', said Edmund Burke. It is the truth of this statement which makes good management such an exacting discipline.

We all achieve most of our learning from experience, but especially from the actions of those above us. Listen carefully next time you hear people talking about their work in the pub, the club or the canteen, and it will not be long before they are discussing what their bosses say and do. The boss is the person who most influences the quality of our lives, second only to our nearest and dearest. How much of what you do now has been learned from observing your immediate superiors in the past?

Attitudes to other individuals in the organisation are particularly infectious. Listen to the way your secretary addresses people on the telephone or greets them when they arrive to see you – those about whom she has heard you make scathing remarks will get different treatment from those she knows you hold in high esteem. She will value the people you value and discount the ones over whom you roll your eyes and sigh when she tells you they called while you were out, or they're waiting to see you. Don't underestimate the wider implications of this fact. The secretarial network can destroy reputations almost overnight.

All the times you have told your staff to treat customers with care and respect will count as naught the first time you deal with a difficult customer and mutter 'silly bitch' under your breath as they walk out of the door.

Socialisation is the process by which we all learn from the examples around us what is the acceptable way to behave in any situation. We learn in this way almost from birth and it is the most potent and lasting form of learning. It is too good to waste and too dangerous to ignore.

Which of the following bad habits could your subordinates be learning from you?

☒ Poor time-keeping, long lunches, or 'missing' for long periods when no one knows where you are or when you will be back. This is discourteous to a secretary or personal assistant anyway, because callers who get an evasive answer from them as to your availability will assume they are ill-informed, disregarded or stupid; and no-one knows that better than the PA.

☒ Delegating unpleasant tasks to others, e.g. informing unsuccessful job interviewees, handling the regular 'pain in the neck' client, carrying out an evening or weekend assignment, or doing duty over the holiday period.

☒ 'Fiddling' expenses, misusing company equipment or supplies, and making personal calls on the office telephone.

☒ Sending staff out in office time to do personal errands for you.

☒ Keeping junior staff waiting when you have arranged to see them, and then letting anyone and everyone interrupt when they are talking to you.

☒ Making disrespectful comments about your boss, or your boss's boss – even in jest. We all know that reveals the greatest truths.

☒ The way you treat customers, clients or patients, but most of all what you say about them afterwards, including non-verbal communications – it takes only one gesture to make a lasting impact.

☒ Interrupting your subordinates' work unnecessarily, and not meeting your own deadlines.

☒ Accepting mediocrity rather than striving for excellence.

Your staff will take their cues from what you do, not what you say.

One sales manager invested a lot of money sending his staff on training courses in telephone technique. He couldn't understand why the effects of the training seemed to wear off after a few weeks, until the company trainer phoned him a couple of times and pointed out to him that whenever he picked up his own phone he just barked 'yes?' into it.

But it is even more effective to use socialisation as a positive force:

☑ Share your own development and learning with your staff, tell them what went well and what didn't, how you might handle it next time, and what you have learned from your experience. When possible, let them observe you at work.

☑ Talk about what you rate as successes; relate the myths of 'greatness' in the organisation, and your staff will learn what is valued and emulate it.

☑ Treat your subordinates as you would like your boss to treat you, and they will treat their own staff the same way.

☑ Share your mistakes (or some of them), and demonstrate how to learn and develop from them.

☑ Keep staff informed on what you are doing, especially on things which relate to their work.

☑ Be enthusiastic about your work and theirs, and about what you are all there to achieve – it is second only to self-interest as a source of influence!

☑ Respect people, time, and the company's goods, and be seen to do so.
☑ Regularly reinforce values and standards by personal contact on the shop-floor, in the typing pool, on the ward or on site.
☑ Maintain high personal standards of honesty and truthfulness, but if it is necessary to be 'economical with the truth', do it yourself, don't delegate it.
☑ If all else fails, ensure you obey the eleventh commandment (Thou shalt not be found out!).

What you do has far more impact on your staff than what you say. But developing staff by example has an even greater subtlety – in the long run, what you do is only as effective as what you believe.

51

Know (and Share) the Customers

Every year, Walt Disney Productions sends its managers out into the field to meet the customers. They put on theme costumes like all their employees and, as Red Pope describes it, 'For a full week, the boss sells tickets or popcorn, dishes ice cream or hot dogs, loads and unloads rides, parks cars, drives the monorail or the trains, and takes on any of 100 on-stage jobs that make the entertainment parks come alive'.

Although the theme of this book is development towards better action through everyday work, there is a danger that we concentrate too heavily on the boss/subordinate relationship and the organisation itself to the exclusion of its customers. Large organisations with a hierarchical structure are particularly prone to the 'incest syndrome'. Employees begin to think they are working for each other's benefit, and that the purpose of the organisation is to provide them with a livelihood and a career. This attitude is reflected in opening or access times, ordering and paying procedures, responses to complaints and change, all of which are geared to the convenience of employees rather than the customer.

The public sector is especially vulnerable to this disease. Because the methods of paying for services are indirect, many local authorities and health boards, for example, don't realise they have 'customers' - only ratepayers and patients who interrupt them at inconvenient times and mess up the ward or make the office look untidy. We all have customers, and disregarding them is the death knell of the organisation, whatever sector it is in.

Whether you manage others who come into direct contact with the customers, or alternatively it is you who does this and your staff act in a supporting, back-room role, you will have to pay particular attention to ensure that customer orientation for both you and your staff is a prime focus in your development activities. If you do not have direct customer contact yourself, it is easy to get out of touch with them and with the day-to-day concerns of your staff.

You can re-establish contact in the following ways:

☑ Spend time regularly at the counter, on site, in the ward, at the reception desk, or with your sales force (anywhere where your people interact directly with customers or clients).

☑ Pick out written or verbal complaints at random and deal with the customer personally, calling on them if necessary.

☑ Be a customer yourself at any of your service points; sample the service but speak and above all listen to the other customers without telling them who you are.

☑ Telephone your own office number a few times and find out how it sounds to a customer. How long does it take you to get hold of the person or service you want? Try the answerphone out of hours too. How off-putting does it sound?

☑ Use customer feedback to generate ideas for change – new products, new services, new forms of delivery. Does your organisation have a free-phone number for customer contact?

☑ Encourage employees to view customers as a source of ideas and to discuss them with you.

☑ Next time the most notorious or offensive 'difficult' customer comes on the line or into the office, deal with him/her yourself, and only then coach your staff on customer-handling techniques.

It may be that you are the person who deals with customers and clients direct while your staff deal with administration, information, production or other related tasks. If so, they need to be kept in touch with your side of the work and to have direct contact with customers regularly if they are to share your goals and aspirations, and improve their own performance. They need to have their efforts reinforced, to see clearly what it is all for, and how their role relates to organisational goals.

☑ Make sure each one of your team regularly accompanies you to meetings, sales conventions, client visits and other situations in which you can share with them the customers and clients with whom you work, and for whom they indirectly work also.

☑ Give them the opportunity to be customers themselves at service points of your own organisation, and your competitors, and review their experience with them afterwards.

☑ Arrange short placements or exchanges between production, administration or support staff and those at service points. Don't forget your secretary in these arrangements – when did he or she last come face to face with a customer?

☑ Employees of any grade and all functions should have direct customer contact at some time. Be creative in making this possible, and include trades union representatives – they need to share commitment to the customer if they are to share the goals of the organisation.

Failing to recognise the customer is a trap many personnel and training specialists fall into. Their immediate customers are the managers and staff of the rest of the organisation (many fail to recognise even this) but they must know and appreciate the needs of the organisation's customers with as much fervour as the most ardent salesperson, dedicated social worker, or inspired refuse collector. As much in production, marketing, or sales, so in housing, planning or education services, the purpose of personnel and training is ultimately to provide the service the customers want to buy or need to have, when and where they want it.

To ensure that you get the best service from the training staff to help you and your team achieve your goals, share the customer with them:

☑ Insist that the training specialists in your organisation meet your customers – take them to see clients, take them on sales trips, or get them to spend time with your staff wherever they are interacting directly with customers.

☑ Invite the trainer to briefings and departmental meetings where you discuss customer needs and your strategy for meeting them.

☑ Share with the trainer customer complaints and queries.

☑ Encourage the trainer to go with you and your staff to try out the services of your competitors and discuss the issues when you return.

☑ Suggest the trainers become customers themselves and try out your sales or service points.

☑ If your customers are intermediary buyers or producers, get the trainer to spend some time on a placement in their organisations.

The benefits you gain from making sure that you know and share the customer far outweigh the time spent. They provide an essential framework to your staff development activities.

52

Read a Chapter Every Week

Introducing staff development is a bit like giving up smoking. Everyone agrees it's a good thing to do, but today never seems to be the right moment. The other similarity is that it is easy enough to start, but more difficult to maintain.

Developing human resources is not an optional extra. The utilisation of every other resource, and the quality and quantity of output in services and products, depends on the people in the organisation. They are the key to success, and no boss, however brilliant as an individual, can achieve very much alone.

The kind of changes in society and technology experienced in the last 10 years will increase in pace and range into the foreseeable future. The resulting complexity and interdependence will give each person greater power of impact on their fellows for good or bad. The potential power of increased technological complexity means that inter-personal relationships and human resource management are more important, not less so.

To cope with this, we need to develop people who are versatile, adaptable, confident, creative and able to sustain their own learning and development throughout their working lives. But this must be done in such a way that we create at the same time a sense of responsibility for shared goals and values.

Staff development must be an integral part of work and management. It should receive the same attention as financial budgeting, production forecasts, acquisition and maintenance of equipment and strategic planning.

The time to start is today, with any chapter in this book. But like all learning, it needs regular reinforcement to maintain momentum, and provide the opportunity for reflection and review of what is working for you. Students who attend time-management courses are invariably full of enthusiasm after the course because it all makes so much sense they can't think why they haven't done all these things before, but, without reinforcement, their good intentions get swept away by everyday routines that prevent them from setting and keeping priorities.

I leave you with the following suggestions:

☑ Read a chapter or two of this book every week to sustain your endeavours. Get others in the organisation to read the book too so that they can share in what you are trying to achieve (but don't lend them this copy – you may not get it back).

☑ Don't let your staff development activities be just a flash in the pan. Be selective as to what will suit you and your team, and plan the time and occasions when you will carry them out. Build in review time too.

☑ It is better not to start too many things at once – pace yourself. If you have done little about developing your people up to now, a sudden onslaught of activity may shock your subordinates and have your boss wondering whether you are suffering from stress.

☑ Try not to reject ideas simply because they have not been done in your organisation before. Take up the opportunity to be innovative. Being confined by preconceived notions of what is possible prevents experimentation and growth of bosses as well as subordinates.

☑ Buy your boss a copy of this book – from the petty cash if necessary!

SOME USEFUL ADDRESSES

Institute of Management
Management House, Cottingham Road, Corby, Northants NN17 1TT
tel: 01536 204222   web: **www.inst-mgt.org.uk**

Confederation of British Industry
Centre Point, 103 New Oxford Street, London, WC1A 1DU
tel: 020 7379 7400 web: **www.cbi.org.uk**

Industrial Society
Peter Runge House, 3 Carlton House Terrace, London, SW1Y 5DG
tel: 020 7479 1000   web: **www.ind.soc.co.uk**

Institute of Manpower Studies
University of Sussex, Mantel Building, Falmer, Brighton BN1 9RF
tel: 01273 606755   web: **www.employment-studies.co.uk**

Chartered Institute of Personnel and Development
CIPD House, Camp Road, London, SW19 4UW
tel: 020 8971 9000   web: **www.cipd.co.uk**

Institute of Supervisory Management
22 Bore Street, Lichfield, Staffordshire, WS13 6LP
tel: 01543 251346   web: **www.ismstowe.com**

National Examination Board for Supervisory and Management Studies (NEBSM)
1 Giltspur Street, London, EC1A 9DD
tel: 020 7294 2470   web: **www.nebsmgt.co.uk**

Trades Union Congress
Congress House, Great Russell Street, London, WC1B 3LS
tel: 020 7636 4030   web: **www.tuc.org.uk**

Workers' Education Association
9 Upper Berkeley Street, London, W1
tel: 020 8983 1515   web: **www.wea.org.uk**

Colleges, business schools, skills centres and other providers of training, materials and advice are usually very content to discuss the types of situations and problems outlined in this book. They may also help to provide books, guides and other literature to help with your research.

Index

Action Learning, 85
Active listening, 147
Aggression, 169
Appraisal, 156
  interview, 157
Assertiveness, 169
Attention to your staff, 42
Authority, 69
Awareness, 105

Barriers to communication, 33
  to listening, 148
Being an example, 210
Bottom-up communication, 162
Brainstorming, 100
Briefing groups, 163

Careers, 24, 108
Career plan, 108
Coaching, 48
Communications, 32
  policy, 164
Competition, 140
Competitiveness, 54
Conflict, 140
Continuing professional development, 138
Counselling, 150
Counsellors, 151
Courses, 181
CPD, 138
Creativity, 98
Customers, 213

Decision preferences, 24
Delegation, 44
Developing yourself, 196
Diary, 18
Direct observation, 58
Disrespect, 167
Distance between boss and staff, 145

Ego states, 35
Employee development plan, 119
Enriching jobs, 68
Enthusiasm, 70
Evaluating training, 181
Exchanges, 65
Experiences, 27

Feedback, 56, 156, 158
Feeling good, 18
Flexibility, 95
Flexi-time, 96

Giving credit, 53
  instruction, 129

Helping rather than telling, 48
High-flyers, 109
High-pressure jobs, 185
How people learn, 27

I'm OK – you 're OK 17
Image building, 201
Induction, 38
Informing and involving, 161
Initial welcome, 40
Instruction, 128
Interference to communication, 32

Job descriptions, 68, 69
Job enrichment, 69

Keeping up to date, 137
Knowing your staff, 21
  yourself, 15

Lack of respect, 167
Leadership, 46
Learning from your subordinates, 175
Learning to instruct, 128

Learning, 28, 178
Learning environment, 178
Learning for action, 84
  log, 199
  preferences, 29
  set, 86
Listening, 147

Managing your boss, 204
Managing conflict, 141
Managing stress, 186
Matching people and jobs, 24
Matrix structure, 78
MBWA, 43, 74
Meetings, 134
Mentoring, 59
Mistakes, 75
Motivation, 103
Mutual Support, 140

Observation, 183
Off-the-job training, 124, 181
'One of the lads', 144

Parent, child, adult, 34
Personal development, 103
  files, 122
  plan, 198
Peter Principle, 62
Preparation for instruction, 129
Preparing for promotion, 62
Prestige, 70
Problem-solving, 28, 69
Professional 'committee' people, 134
Professional and technical institutes, 138
Project teams, 78

Quality Circles, 90
Questionnaires, 183

Recording progress, 121
Record-keeping, 121
Recruitment advertising, 39
Relationships, 60
Reputation, 201

Resource library, 138
Respect, 166
Responsibility, 69
Rewards, 53

Secondments, 65
Self-development, 196
Self-evaluation, 105
Self-knowledge, 15
Smiling, 208
Socialisation, 210
Socialising, 144
Sources of stress, 188
Staff development, 24
Standards, 46
Stereotypes, 95
Strengths and weaknesses, 158
Stress, 185
Stretching abilities, 72
Stroking, 42
Succession planning, 63
Symptoms of stress, 186

Taking risks, 75
Talent, 73
  spotting, 74
Team briefing, 134
Technological change, 137
Testing/simulation, 183
Time management, 191
Time-planning, 194
Time-saving, 192
Trainers, 112
Training and development, 115
  evaluation, 182
  plan, 117
Transactional Analysis, 34
Trust, 69

Visual Aids, 131

Working at home, 96
Work-shedding, 193

Zen Buddhism, 15